WHY CLEVER PEOPLE
DO DUMB THINGS

9 STEPS TO HELP YOU FEEL AS SUCCESSFUL ON THE INSIDE AS YOU APPEAR ON THE OUTSIDE

LINDSAY SPENCER-MATTHEWS

WHY CLEVER PEOPLE DO DUMB THINGS
9 steps to help you feel as successful on the inside as you appear on the outside

© 2015 LINDSAY SPENCER-MATTHEWS

ISBN: 978 0 9942325 0 2

Editor: Jacqueline Pretty The Grammar Factory

Cover image © Svinkin/Shutterstock
Cover design by Fiaz Ahmed Irfan
Internal design and typesetting by Tanya Edbrooke

Printed in Australia by The Printing Office, Eagle Farm, Queensland

Copies of this book may be obtained from www.greatchangemaker.com.au

#CleverPeople
Web – www.greatchangemaker.com.au
Email - info@greatchangemaker.com.au
Facebook – GreatChangeMaker
Twitter – Gr8ChangeMaker
LinkedIn – Lindsay Spencer-Matthews

GREAT
((CHANGE))
MAKER

Dedicated to my wonderful wife, Sarah.
Without your help, support, and encouragement
this book would not have happened,
neither would life as I now know it.

WHY CLEVER PEOPLE
DO DUMB THINGS

The title of this book is (just like the contents) inspired and inspiring. This book gives you a powerful framework and structure to transform and totally enrich your life. And it very simply lets you share that enrichment with others through Lindsay's partnership with B1G1: Business for Good. Just the simple act of buying this great book makes a real difference in the lives of people in need around the world. And that is one very, very clever thing to do too.

Paul Dunn | Co-Founder and Chairman

I hope you enjoy this book. I wrote it to inform, entertain, and hopefully change your life.

Regardless of your experience reading this book I hope you can feel good in the knowledge that your ownership of it has contributed towards the relieving of a young woman's suffering somewhere in the world.

We are proud to be B1G1 (Buy1Give1: Business for Good) partners and have committed that every one of these books we sell or gift will aid in the rehabilitation of a girl rescued from commercial sexual exploitation by sponsoring one meal for one day. A nutritious meal feeds not only the physical body, but also nourishes the soul of the beneficiary. This contribution will allow these girls to go through academic and job skills training, giving them a new lease of life and enable them to be independent earning members of their families. On their behalf, thanks.

Lindsay Spencer-Matthews | Great Change Maker

V

9 STEPS TO HELP YOU FEEL AS SUCCESSFUL ON THE INSIDE AS YOU APPEAR ON THE OUTSIDE

R RECOGNISE WHO'S REALLY IN CONTROL

E EVALUATE YOUR REALITY GAP

A ALIGN WITH YOUR VALUES

N NUDGE YOUR AUTO PILOT

I INFLUENCE YOUR CLEVER BRAIN

M MANAGE YOUR AUTO PILOT

A ACTIVATE YOUR CLEVER BRAIN TO CHANGE YOUR LIFE

T TRAIN OTHERS TO INFLUENCE YOUR AUTO PILOT

E ENJOY A RICH, FULL AND MEANINGFUL LIFE

CONTENTS

INTRODUCTION

Look out – you are about to read a book that's going to change your life … deliberately!

If you feel that there is nothing that needs to change in your life, please stop reading right now. If you are such a person then you need to be *writing* a book, not reading one. You are an incredibly rare human being. Your life must be one of almost indescribable daily joy. You have taken the rough diamond of your life and polished it to a brilliant gem. Or perhaps you just appreciate the shapeless lump of your life and don't want it to become a diamond. Either way, congratulations. In the words of Star Trek's Mr Spock, 'Live long and prosper'.

However, if you're like most of the people I see in my practice, that probably isn't the case. You are most likely one of those people who feels a confused dissatisfaction with your life. You feel frustrated and limited, but might not know why. You probably appear happy on the outside, but on the inside you are struggling. If you are in a loving relationship, you might feel a distance between the two of you, or perhaps you find yourself getting irritated by silly little things. If you're in a not-so-loving relationship, you're staying because you can't think of a way out. If you have kids then you may find yourself feeling really frustrated as a parent, and often saying things you later regret. You may find yourself infuriated by the selfishness and stupidity you see in other people to the point of 'going postal'. Overall, if you rated your wellbeing on a scale of 1-100, with 1 being the lowest a person's wellbeing could be and 100 being the highest, it would be below 60. If you really think about it, then it is very likely that you will feel a sense of being 'out of control'.

You probably look around you and see other people who seem luckier, richer, happier, and generally much better off than you – and they're not even as intelligent as you!

Having said all that, you also have strong values, morals, and principles. Some of the things you have done in your life haunt you because you cannot understand how you could do such stupid, selfish, impulsive, and downright harmful things. In other words – you are a normal human being.

So if you're a normal human being, does that mean dissatisfaction's just part of the human condition? Should you just give up?

Not at all. You probably haven't noticed it, but you are changing your life every day. The only issue is that, until now, you've been doing it by accident (hence the dissatisfaction). Once you have read this book all that will change. You will notice things differently. You will act and react differently. You will think differently, and you will think about the way you think differently. You will have moved from being an 'Accidental You' to an 'Intentional You'.

ACCIDENTAL VERSUS INTENTIONAL

You have spent your entire life evolving into the person you are today. However, almost all of the effort you have expended to become the person you are right now has been accidental and invisible to you. As an example, I have *never* met a client who has been able to identify a time that they deliberately decided to become angry, depressed or anxious.

This means that this unhappy, dissatisfied and helpless you is the Accidental You. This book is about becoming the Intentional You.

The Intentional You feels content and satisfied with life. The Intentional You makes decisions that are in line with your values. The Intentional You ensures you are treated with respect, and treats others with respect. While life isn't perfect, the Intentional You acknowledges and appreciates everything that *does* work, and consciously chooses to change the things that *don't* work in your life.

And what can you expect by becoming this Intentional You?

Consider the *Titanic*, the most famous maritime disaster in history. In order to have missed the iceberg the *Titanic* did not need to engage in a 180-degree change of direction. It needed to travel slightly slower, and change course by one or two degrees in a timely and deliberate manner. Had it done so then its future, and the future of all of those people who perished and the lives of those they touched, would have changed in unimaginable ways.

The *Titanic* is an example of life events overtaking real values. The generally held belief regarding that tragedy is that the captain was instructed to make the fastest time to New York. In order to meet this instruction he overcame his better judgement and travelled at a speed which, with the wisdom of hindsight, placed the entire vessel in peril. This book is a call for you to take your own values (read – better judgement) into consideration rather than unwittingly allowing external influences and habitual behaviours to influence you to do things which you later regret. It will involve the expenditure of some effort and intent, but so does apologising for those times when we act contrary to our values and engage in behaviours that we almost immediately regret.

The *Titanic* is an apt metaphor for human change, in that the degree of change that is typically needed to reduce the number of dumb things you do and increase the number of clever things that you do is almost always very small. This book is not an attempt to change you profoundly; it is an attempt to change *your life* profoundly. This will happen by changing the way you think about the way you think and allowing you to react in a way that is closer to your values.

While this book will not make you happy, rich, worry-free, or better looking, and it cannot fix other people, reduce your mortgage, or give you next week's lotto numbers, it will change the way you think about the way you think. It will give you a very different world view of yourself, your thoughts, feelings, and actions, and others who influence your life. This book will be the catalyst, a change agent.[1]

How do I know this?

In my journey as a person and a psychologist I have spent a huge amount of time trying to work out why people (including me!) do the things they do. I discovered in my mid-thirties that I was an intelligent person. Until that time I had held the belief that the stupid things I had done in my life were evidence that I was a stupid person.

After drifting through a twenty-year career in sales and marketing, and having experienced two significant relationship failures, I became a registered psychologist in 1994. I have been in amateur theatrical productions, I was the lead singer in a rock band, and I have lectured and tutored in university to Master's level. Before becoming a psychologist I successfully sold everything from medical products to real estate. Since I became a psychologist I have created a network of psychologists working in medical practices, owned a small business, driven a truck, and been involved in network marketing.

---

1. In secondary school my science teacher brought into class a large glass container of a pink liquid. I have no idea what it was to this day. She then introduced us to the idea of a catalyst. Taking an eye-dropper, she dripped a single drop of a clear solution onto the pink liquid. At a rate slow enough to clearly observe, the pink liquid miraculously changed into a clear liquid. We were all singularly impressed with this transformation.

    We discovered in that class that the catalyst facilitates the change without being consumed by it. In other words, the initial substances undergo a chemical change which would not have happened as quickly, or at all, without the catalyst, while the catalyst remains intact.

I retired in 2002 having made a million dollars in property, and returned to the workforce in 2007 having lost it all. As Paul Kelly sang, 'I've done all the dumb things'. Thankfully I have also done some things that are not so dumb, and I hope to share some of them with you in this book.

Reflecting on my own experience and others' behaviours led me to realise that everyone does stupid things, things that are contrary to their values, and things that demonstrate double standards.

In my early career as a psychologist I discovered that Cognitive Behaviour Therapy (CBT) was an attempt to identify those maladaptive behaviours and develop techniques to moderate them. Unfortunately the complexity of human behaviour, and of CBT, meant that many of my counselling clients found it hard to implement and sustain within their own life circumstances. And if implementing CBT was too difficult, I knew I had to find a solution that my clients found easy to work with in their own lives.

I enthusiastically explored a range of therapies and added a range of acronyms to my qualifications, including (but not an exhaustive list!) RET, DBT, EMDR, EFT and ISTDP. Each of these had value and contributed to my skill as a therapist, but a clear model of why smart people continued to do things that left them unhappy and dissatisfied with their lives still eluded me.

Then I began to explore Acceptance and Commitment Theory (ACT). In simple terms, ACT is a model which aims to help people engage in a more mindful appreciation of their behaviours, to disconnect their emotions from their experiences, and to move closer to their values. ACT fitted my beliefs and experiences like a hand fitting into a glove, and I knew it had the potential to help a lot of people get unstuck so that they could move on in their lives and open up their horizons. ACT allowed me to begin to REANIMATE myself and my clients. Now I hope that it can help to REANIMATE you.

When I re-entered private practice in 2011 I began measuring my counselling performance statistically. I began to realise that there were recurring elements of my practice, elements which were highly effective. The doctors who referred to me were consistently doing so, and my clients were responding in a reasonably short number of sessions. I was making a real difference in clients' lives.

As I began to mindfully notice these trends, a metaphor started to emerge. This metaphor changed the way my clients think about the way they think, it shattered their illusion of being 'in control', and gave them the tools they needed to take back some of their control and change themselves and their lives for the better. And it all started with the idea that you have two brains … but more on that in *Chapter 1*.

ABOUT THIS BOOK

This book will teach you to deliberately influence your own thoughts, actions and language so that you can have a more rich, full and meaningful life.

The framework of this book revolves around nine steps that have emerged from my work with thousands of clients. To try to make these nine steps more accessible I have used the acronym REANIMATE which, while sometimes a little laboured, has very real relevance. This acronym is meant to acknowledge that you have been asleep at the wheel of your life for a long time, and this process will reawaken/REANIMATE you. It is designed to activate a seldom used part of your brain – the part of your brain which makes you a clever person and reduces the likelihood of doing dumb things.

In the early stages after reading this book you will struggle to overcome some of the entrenched behaviours which you find so vexatious just after they happen. However, as you continue

WHY CLEVER PEOPLE DO DUMB THINGS

practicing, you will ultimately find that you are engaging in the process more and more spontaneously until it becomes a way of life.

Ultimately, you will awaken resources and capabilities that have been quiescent for most of your life.

DISCLAIMER

The information outlined in this book is designed to help you change your life in alignment with your own desires and values. However, I need to warn you of two things before we get started.

The first is that the change process can be unpredictable, and that I cannot recall a client who had a clear vision of what they expected from the process other than to change the things that weren't working. The only promise that I can make regarding change is that this process works within the boundaries of your own values. The likelihood of any change generated through this process being contrary to your values is very small. One reality of exploring and deliberately working within your values is that some outcomes may require legitimate compromise, which can bring difficult decisions.

The second is that you must have a willingness to change. It is not uncommon in therapy to meet with clients who would be happier remaining in their current state of misery than risk change. This is exemplified by a lovely story about a man who moved to a new neighbourhood and, on his first day walking to the bus to work, passed a nearby house. On the veranda of the house lay an old dog which was clearly in great discomfort. It whined and whuffled piteously. As an animal lover this preyed on the man's mind all day so he retraced his route on the way home, only to find the dog still there and still seemingly miserable. The man summoned his courage, walked up to the house, and rang the bell. When the dog owner answered the door the passer-by apologised for intruding, expressed his concern over the dog's wellbeing, and offered to help if he could. The owner laughed and explained that the dog was whining because where it sat on the porch there was a big nail sticking up. Incredulously the passer-by asked, 'Why doesn't he move?' The owner replied, 'Because the nail isn't hurting him enough yet!'

It is the intent of this book to help you engage in a change process which will be in line with your own desires and values. There are already aspects of your life which are brilliant, functional and worthwhile. It is unlikely that these things will change to any significant degree. Instead, this book will alert you to the nails which are contributing to your misery, and motivate you to take deliberate action to move to another place on the porch, to fix the nail, or to accept that the pain of the nail is offset by the advantages of sitting there!

I am proud to present this book to you, and I hope that it brings you closer to a rich, full and meaningful life.

Cheers,
Lindsay

CHAPTER 1:

RECOGNISE WHO'S REALLY IN CONTROL

Who do you think is in control of what you do,

and think,

and say?

Whenever I put this question to my clients, some identify other people or their environment as being in control. Now, while other people and the environment are *influencing* factors, they are not control factors.

If a police officer puts a hand up to stop me then she is influencing me, not controlling me. It is my choice to accept her influence and stop. However, if I chose to, then I *could* run over her. Happily my values include being a law abiding citizen so I would allow the police officer to influence my behaviour. If, on the other hand, I was a career criminal and the consequences of stopping included going to jail, then the likelihood of me being influenced by the police officer would reduce and I might accelerate, regardless of the escalation of my already parlous circumstances.

So, back to the question of control. At this point in the conversation the overwhelming majority of clients readily state that they are in control of their lives. This assertion is made in spite of the fact that they are sitting in a psychologist's office seeking outside help because they feel they are *not* in control!

What these clients are reporting is the 'Illusion of Control'. This illusion is universal, invisible and almost overwhelming. In exploring this illusion I ask clients to think about which shoe they put on first when they get dressed. The usual answers are 'I don't know', 'my left one', or 'my right one'. None of them are evidence of the person being in control of what they do. 'I don't know' is evidence of their environment determining which shoe they put on first, and 'my left/right one' is evidence that their habits make the decision. I often ask them how successful they would be if they decided, just for thirty days, to put their other shoe on first each time they dress. Most smile and admit that they might be okay for a day or so, but that the demands of everyday life will soon overtake them and they will lapse back into their original habit. This is a small but powerful example of the Illusion of Control.

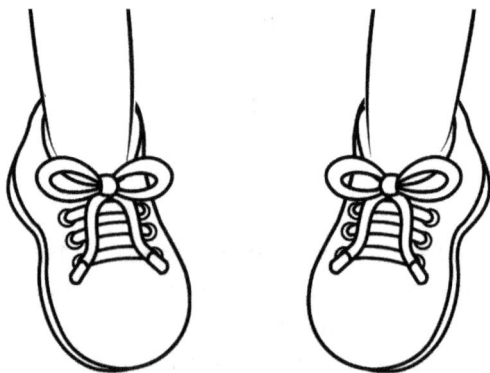

Another demonstration of the Illusion of Control is driving a car. Most people maintain that they are in control of the vehicle when they drive. Please consider the last time you drove a car. Did you actually pay any attention to the angle at which your right foot rested on the accelerator? Or where the indicator stalk was every time you made a turn? Almost every road user has had the experience of arriving at their destination and suddenly realising that they have no recollection of the actual journey. This is relatively normal behaviour and clearly demonstrates that most of the complex and dangerous tasks involved in driving a car are automated.

WHY DOES THIS HAPPEN?

It comes down to how our brains are wired. And this wiring is a result of the way our experiences have 'programmed' us.

Essentially, we repeat certain behaviours so many times that they become programmed into our brains. This means that whenever we encounter circumstances that trigger one of these programs we respond in the way we always have. If we hear the words 'What is two times two?' we respond with 'Four!' We don't stop to solve a mathematical equation, the response is already programmed. Likewise, we don't think about which shoe to put on first each morning – that response has also been programmed.

Now this isn't always a bad thing. In fact, habitual behaviours can be really helpful in that they are designed to reduce the number of decisions we need to make, thereby allowing us to focus on the really important things. I definitely don't consider deliberately deciding which shoe you put on first to be part of a rich, full, and meaningful life. This is vitally important – otherwise getting dressed would take adults as long as it takes a three-year-old (or a teenager!). The automation of repeated, simple, and mundane behaviours is incredibly valuable. It is also incredibly effective. This is really helpful and highly functional as long as it works.

A CLEVER BRAIN EXERCISE...

Take some time over the next few days to notice how much of what you do, and think, and say without having to think first. My expectation is that you will be staggered by how much of your life is automated. I also hope that you will be amazed at how much of it actually *works!*

But what happens when it doesn't work?

One of the interesting things to note about our automatic behaviour is that every one of us has had the experience of having a 'wakeup call', where we were jarred out of our automatic behaviours and we actively then question those behaviours. When something interesting, alarming, or important comes up, a very clever part of our brilliant brain (called the Reticular Activating System) wakes us up. However, when nothing out of the ordinary occurs you can easily get stuck in the same behaviours, and some of them might not be ones that help you create the type of life you want, or become the type of person you want to be.

In my case, my early driving habits were influenced by the difficulty that the authorities had in detecting speeding drivers. For my first twenty years of driving there were no speed cameras or other clever and effective ways to catch me. I was also a young punk who had some rally driving experience and held the (ridiculous) belief that I was as safe at 75kph as everyone else was at 60kph. Every couple of years I would be detected and I considered the fines to be a 'speeding tax' which I was happy to pay. I make this self-disclosure in the full knowledge that it casts me in a very poor light. I also make it in the realisation that I was on 'Auto Pilot' for all of that time and did not realise it. Even when lectured and fined by the police for speeding, I still maintained my ridiculous belief that my actions were rational and reasonable!

Your brain works in the same way, and you carry out a series of habitual behaviours every day that have been programmed by your experiences. Habitual actions like getting dressed and driving a car are just one example of how we really aren't in control of our actions.

The other area I'd like to look at is *losing* control.

Simply reflect on your recent past to identify whether or not you have said or done something which you later regretted. The 'normal' response to this reflection is a self-deprecating 'yes', which is seemingly clear evidence that you were not in control at that moment.

Believe it or not, this is a result of the same programming. Road rage is the perfect example. The victim rarely sets out to deliberately enrage another driver. It is common for road rage to be initiated by the victim asserting their perception of their 'rights' on the road, or perhaps attempting to communicate to the other driver that their behaviour is unreasonable. The perpetrator then demonstrates classic 'out of control' behaviour. Both the victim's and the perpetrator's behaviour are based on conclusions they've drawn from their own experiences and beliefs (our programming). In short, both of them think they are right.

To return to my driving experience, this 'dumb' behaviour was demonstrated when technology caught up with me. I vividly recall in 1989 receiving my first photographic speeding fine in the mail. I was incredulous, disbelieving, and outraged! It had to be a mistake. The idea that I was clever and skilled enough to speed safely (yes, that is an oxymoron!) and observant enough to avoid speed traps was so ingrained that I invested the required $10 and duly received a colour photo of myself, in my driver's seat, doing 71kph in a 60kph zone.

Until then, my behaviour had 'worked' for me, and perpetuated the Illusion of Control. And this is the case for most people – in most people's lives the overwhelming number of these programmed behaviours and avoidances are functional, meaning they work. This invisibly leads us into the Illusion of Control, along with the sense that we are *right*, making our own, and others', unworkable behaviour confusing, offending, or even infuriating!

When a behaviour stops 'working' for us (or we realise a behaviour has never worked for us), something needs to change.

In my case, I paid the fine and, I am a little proud to say, reviewed my habitual driving behaviours. In the twenty-four years since I have had three more camera fines and I take personal responsibility for all of them. Each and every time I have clearly not been 'in control' of my vehicle. Over those twenty-four years I have used all sorts of clever devices to decrease the chances of my exceeding the speed limit, including speed alarms, cruise control, and very recently the TomTom app on my iPhone. I use this example in an attempt to demonstrate that, regardless of how intent we are on influencing our behaviour so that it reflects our values, we will all still make mistakes. This book is *not* about how to have a perfect life; it is how to have a rich, full, and meaningful life – mistakes and all!

So who's really in control?

As my new behaviours emerged and my driving became more skilful, legal, and safe, I continued to try to figure out why unworkable behaviours are so common. As I further explored ACT I began to form the belief that one explanation of human behaviour might lie in a metaphor...

You have two brains. No, really. Let me explain.

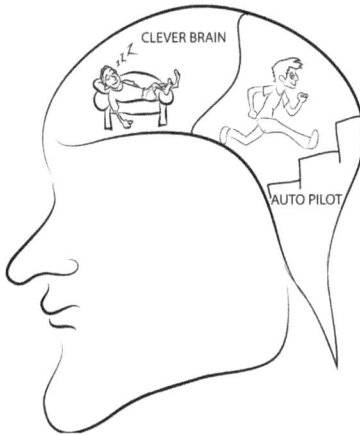

Several years ago I began to experiment with the idea that human behaviour could be explained by imagining that we had two separate brains. While this is clearly not the case physiologically, there is still some physiological support for the idea. We all have the large wrinkly bit at the top of our brain, which is almost completely absent in other animals. This cerebral cortex is the part of our brain where most 'higher-order' functions are carried out. In short, it's our 'Clever Brain'.

I began to wonder what role in our day-to-day lives this Clever Brain might play. I considered the fact that when people engage in behaviours which 'don't work', those behaviours seem to be illogical, are often contrary to a sense of moral 'right', cause rather than solve problems, do not match the person's values, and almost always carry undesirable consequences. This led me to conclude that the Clever Brain is the place where logic, moral rectitude, problem solving, values, and a sense of the consequences of our actions might live.

I also considered the function of the part of the brain where programmed behaviours and programmed avoidances lived. I now call this part of the brain our 'Auto Pilot'. The actual physiology of the brain lends itself to the idea that this is the 'lizard brain' that rests atop our spinal column, nestled underneath the Clever Brain (this is the part of the brain we share with other animals, unlike our relatively huge cerebral cortex). I imagined that this part of the brain might be where our habits live, where our emotions are generated, where we'd find the basis of our personality, and that it might manage our body via the autonomic nervous system. Now I admit, this metaphor is not scientifically robust from a physiological perspective. As a psychological explanation it does, however, go a long way to explaining why and how we do some of the perplexing things we do.

As I further examined this metaphor, I wondered what the limitations of each 'brain' might be.

My approach relates to the early days of my career when I was working in organisational psychology. The relationship between management and workers fascinated me, and I have found a parallel with the two brains model. I now imagine that my Clever Brain is the intelligent but lazy manager, and my Auto Pilot is an incredibly motivated, energetic, capable, but stupid employee.

The Auto Pilot is an incredibly capable brain once it has been taught to do something. Did you pay any attention to chewing your food when you last ate? Do you ever reflect on the miracle of walking? These are everyday examples of your Auto Pilot doing things invisibly for you which usually work.

Unfortunately, our Auto Pilot lacks the ability to work out whether or not the things it does are functional or not. After all, why else would he[2] repeat behaviour which clearly does not work? If our Auto Pilot could actually hear when someone we love or respect is talking, then how many arguments would we be able to avoid? If our Auto Pilot could see, then how could we ignore speed signs? If our Auto Pilot could speak then how would he not ask us for clarification? And if he could think then surely we would not do things that do not work for us. These considerations led me to conclude that our Auto Pilot is deaf, mute, blind, and stupid. The fact that it is such a brilliant 'doing' machine deludes us into believing that we are acting intelligently when we are acting in accordance with habits rather than acting with deliberate intent.

Auto Pilot	Clever Brain
Attributes	
Habitual behaviours	Logic
Emotions	Moral right from wrong
Personality	Creative problem solving
Physical reactions	Values
	Consequences
Limitations	
Deaf	Cannot "do" anything spontaneously
Mute	Lazy
Blind	
Stupid (dumb)	

This table can be a handy reference as you awaken your Clever Brain and retrain your Auto Pilot. As you read through the coming chapters, keep these attributes and limitations in mind.

To further illustrate the role and abilities of the Auto Pilot, consider the following piece of prose, which made the hairs on my arms stand up on my first read. I offer it to you in the hope that you might answer the question at the end with 'I am your Auto Pilot'.

---

2. For ease of use, I will refer to the Auto Pilot as 'he' and 'him', but there is no rule relating to Auto Pilot gender. Feel free to determine for yourself whether yours is male or female.

Who am I?

I am your constant companion.

I am your greatest helper or heaviest burden.

I will push you onward or drag you down to failure.

I am completely at your command.

Half the things you do you might just as well turn over to me, and I will be able to do them quickly, correctly.

I am easily managed – you must merely be firm with me. Show me exactly how you want something done, and after a few lessons I will do it automatically.

I am the servant of all great people; and alas, of all failures as well. Those who are failures, I have made failures.

I am not a machine, though I work with all the precision of a machine plus the intelligence of a human being.

You may run me for a profit or turn me for ruin – it makes no difference to me.

Take me, train me, be firm with me, and I will place the world at your feet.

Be easy with me and I will destroy you.

Who am I? I am habit.

– *Anonymous*

Consider mathematics. Most of us can instantly respond with the correct answer when asked 'What is two times two?' When I ask my clients this, almost everyone instantly responds with the correct answer of 'four'. When I then ask 'What is four times four?' Around half the time clients respond with the answer 'eight'. I then repeat the question and they always look sheepish and provide the correct answer. I then ask 'What is the square root of nine?' A very small number of people are able to provide the answer immediately. A slightly larger proportion is able to deliberately work out the answer, and most struggle until we discuss what 'square root' means. The majority are then able to calculate the right answer. Very occasionally I get to the final question in the series which is 'What is the fourth prime number?' The overwhelming majority are unable to work this out but, when informed as to what a prime number is[3], most can work it out.

These are clear examples of the two brains at work. Whenever a question is immediately answered then the work has been done by the Auto Pilot. When a prompt is required which then immediately results in the right answer then it is, again, the Auto Pilot demonstrating that its power of rote recall is not perfect. When the answer is a struggle requiring actual calculation, then it is the work of the Clever Brain.

---

3. A prime number is a whole number greater than one which can only be divided by itself or the number one without leaving a remainder. Have you worked out the answer yet?
   Check out my website www.greatchangemaker.com.au/CleverPeople.

How our Auto Pilot influences our behaviour

In their book *The Weight Escape*, Ciarrochi, Bailey and Harris introduced a clever representation of the way our behaviours are influenced by our Auto Pilot. Called the 'Choice Point worksheet', I have adapted this simple and elegant diagram to include my two brain metaphor, and will refer to it as the Influence Diagram throughout this book.

First, let's examine the Choice Point worksheet:

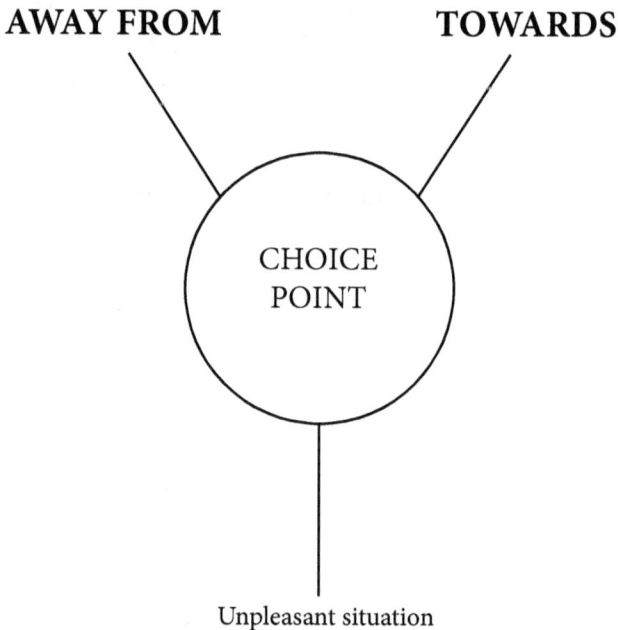

AWAY FROM   **TOWARDS**

CHOICE
POINT

Unpleasant situation

This diagram shows us that our behaviour is typically a response to the situations in our lives, and the Choice Point is when we choose those behaviours. The authors propose that a 'mindful pause' at the Choice Point can be where we reflect on our values, and where conflicting habitual and emotional responses will influence whether our behaviour moves us towards, or away from our values.

In the case of situations that frequently arise (such as our shoes being on a certain side of the chair when we put them on in the morning), these situations program our habitual behaviours (meaning we always put on a certain shoe first). Our Clever Brain then delegates these behaviours to our Auto Pilot. Once this happens, we are almost always at the mercy of these behaviours and we are susceptible to doing dumb things.

I believe this means the idea of the Choice Point is moot.

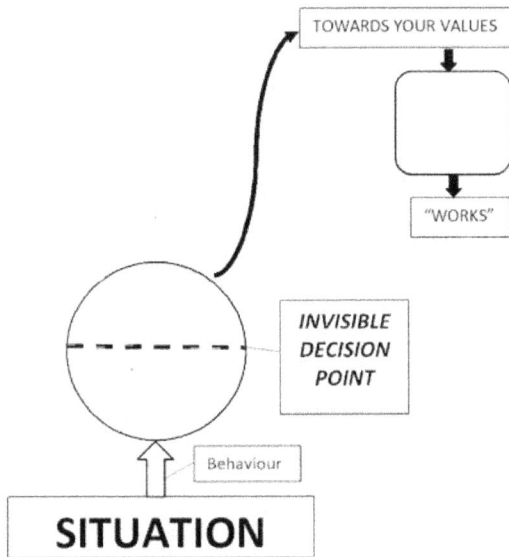

If we temporarily omit the Choice Point and continue with the emergence of behaviour, there are really only two ways that our behaviour can progress, either 'towards' or 'away from' our desired outcomes – as demonstrated in the previous diagram. Behaviour that leads us 'towards' our desired outcomes is behaviour that 'works', while behaviour that leads us 'away from' those outcomes is behaviour that 'doesn't work'.

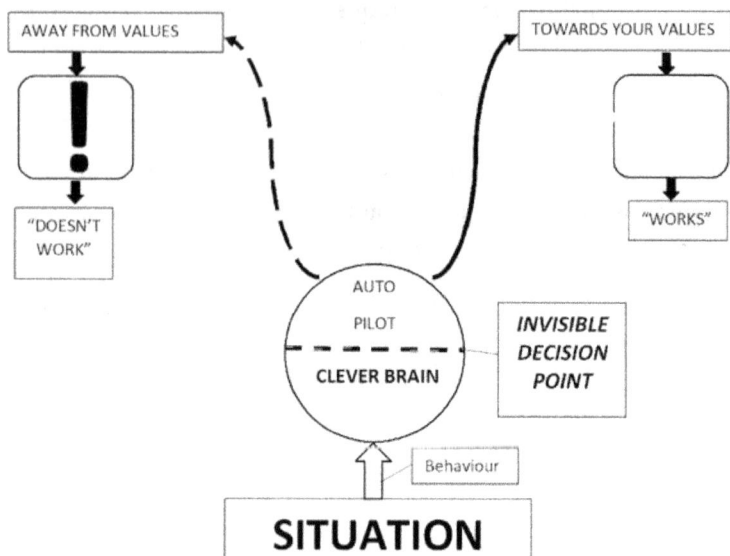

AWAY FROM VALUES		TOWARDS YOUR VALUES

"DOESN'T WORK"

"WORKS"

AUTO
PILOT
- - - -
CLEVER BRAIN

INVISIBLE
DECISION
POINT

Behaviour

SITUATION

Here we see the behaviour emerging from the situation and leading towards our values. This is the definition of clever behaviour.

It is my argument that these clever behaviours are almost always 'invisible' in that we do not notice them. When was the last time you congratulated yourself on getting your shoes onto the right feet, or having successfully driven your car to the local store?

When I play tennis and return a high ball above my head while running backwards and actually win the point it is *not* a demonstration of me being in 'control' of the shot. When such shots do work (tragically rare in my case!) it is because I have relinquished control to pre-programmed behaviours and those behaviours are up to the task at hand. The most I have control over is my desire to make the ball land in the desired place on the other side of the court.

But, what happens when our behaviour takes us away from our values?

Unlike when our behaviour *does* work, when our behaviour *doesn't* work it is usually immediately apparent to us. That is because this behaviour stimulates our Reticular Activating System which wakes up our Clever Brain in response to the alarming, unusual or important turn of events.

Whether we have stumbled on the stairs, incorrectly positioned our fingers on the keyboard and typed gobbledegook, or found ourselves daydreaming in an important meeting at work, our Clever Brain is often rudely jolted awake. The exclamation mark in the diagram indicates our awareness of this 'unworkable' behaviour, which then leads us to a moment of realisation, otherwise known as an 'Oh no!' moment. (Many clients have a more eloquent label for this moment, but in print I would prefer to keep it clean.)

THE INVISIBLE DECISION POINT

Before you act, there is an 'Invisible Decision Point'. This is the instant in time where, if you were in control of what you do, think and say, you would act in a way that moves you towards your values, rather than away from them.

While this Invisible Decision Point is the moment when real control over our behaviour is exercised, it is almost never exercised with our deliberate intent. Unlike the Choice Point, which implies that we are in control and making deliberate decisions, I prefer to call this the Invisible Decision Point, simply because any decision made by our Auto Pilot is invisible (at least, until we have an 'Oh no!' moment and have to deal with the consequences). This is the moment when our Auto Pilot instantaneously looks through its vast repertoire of habitual behaviours and selects the one which it feels fits the requirements of the moment – whether it works or not!

This highlights the fact that we are not in control – the decision regarding which direction our behaviour has gone has been the responsibility of our Auto Pilot.

As a normal person, your Auto Pilot makes thousands of these Invisible Decisions every day. The overwhelming majority of them move to the right side of the worksheet, and virtually all of them are invisible to you because they work. In fact, if they were not invisible to you it is unlikely that you could successfully endure or survive your day. Do you really want to be in control when you run down a flight of stairs? Or touch type? Or form a sentence in response to your boss's request for an update on the status of that project you are working on? Okay, maybe you do need some degree of control for the last one but I know for a fact that the moment I try to 'control' my use of the racquet on the tennis court I start missing the ball entirely.

It is my contention that the decisions that 'work' can be left as they are. After all, they're already working courtesy of our Auto Pilot! They are an example of our dumb brain doing clever things. There is unlikely to be a reality gap when our automated behaviours 'work'.

Instead, what you want is to prevent those 'Oh no!' moments from happening. And the first step is to become more conscious of those 'Oh no!' moments or, in other words, to figure out what's not working. This represents the first element of the REANIMATE process – recognise who's really in control.

Chapter Summary

- The illusion of control is universal and invisible.
- In reality our habits control almost everything we do.
- The part of our brain which controls our lives lacks any real insight or intelligence.
- Our higher order thought processes can be deliberately activated to influence our habitual behaviours.

CHAPTER 2:

EVALUATE YOUR REALITY GAP

Lewis Carroll's *Alice in Wonderland* introduced us to the character of the Cheshire Cat. This strange creature told Alice that if she did not know where she was going, then it did not matter which way she went. We're going to take that idea one step further.

The purpose of this book is to lead you to a more rich, full and meaningful life by retraining your Auto Pilot and awakening your Clever Brain. But if you don't know where you are now, then how will you know you have actually changed?

In my private psychology practice I almost always take benchmark data at the beginning of the first session, progress data at the beginning and end of every session, and closure data at the final session. I owe this habit to Scott Miller, an influencing force worldwide on the subject of effectiveness in therapy, and his excellent Outcome Rating Scale (ORS) and Session Rating Scale (SRS).

These tools are available online free of charge so visit scottdmiller. com/performance-metrics/ to download a personal copy. The ORS measures and helps you plot your feelings of satisfaction with life in general on a scale of 1 to 40, with 1 being very low wellbeing and 40 being very high. Any score below 25 is considered evidence of some psychological distress.

The benefit of regularly measuring your overall satisfaction is that you have evidence of any improvements. When working with clients, I'm aware that the therapeutic process is often an incremental one and gains are often not noticed until the ORS is reviewed over time. Without offering benchmarking of some kind, therapy is open to either frustration at a perceived lack of progress, or of having its perceived effectiveness inflated by a client wanting to give positive feedback to their therapist after a rewarding session. While the ORS is no real guarantee of overcoming these limitations, it does offer some form of measurement.

You can also acknowledge your Auto Pilot for the new habits he has created, which have led to this increased satisfaction (more on this in *Chapter 6*), or if you find your satisfaction dropping, you will realise very quickly and then can use your Clever Brain to redirect your Auto Pilot to return to an upward trajectory.

A CLEVER BRAIN EXERCISE...

Visit scottdmiller.com/performance-metrics/ to complete Scott's ORS. Record your results and reflect on them as you work through this book to measure the progress you make.

CASE STUDY

Last year Michael (not the client's real name) was referred to me by his GP for treatment relating to long-term depression. According to my usual practice I asked Michael to complete the ORS and he reported his wellbeing as 20/40 (below the benchmark for psychological distress of 25/40).

Michael had been struggling for over a decade following a series of significant illnesses and life events. He and I engaged in a therapeutic relationship which, in my practice experience, was unusually long. After six sessions Michael expressed his belief that he was not getting any better. I reviewed his records and drew him a graph of his ORS scores over the sessions to date. The graph (shown below) demonstrated a clear and encouraging growth from his initial 20/40 to 28/40. This evidence of improvement, which had been invisible to Michael before this conversation, bolstered his belief in his own ability to make meaningful change in his life, and sustained him for the next *stage in his recovery. Without that numerical and regular measure of his improvement, Michael would have been very likely to have lost heart and potentially to have relapsed into the* depression which had troubled him for so long.

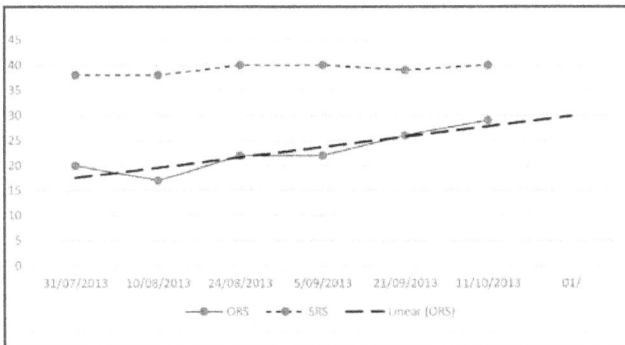

If you are already working with a therapist then consider introducing the ORS and SRS to them.[4] If they are not amenable to such an idea, then perhaps you could use the measures independently. If the results are in line with your expectations of the therapeutic process, then no harm has been done. If you find that these empirical (numeric) measures cause you to question the effectiveness of the work you are doing, then you can make a more informed judgement of the process and the therapist, and perhaps even have an informed conversation with them as to why you would continue using their services.

THE REALITY GAP

An important aspect of last chapter's Influence Diagram is the idea of things that 'work' and things that 'don't work'. While the ORS and SRS are useful tools for getting an overview of your progress, to take independent action you need to have a clear picture or what is and isn't working in your life.

As you now know, most people unwittingly allow their Auto Pilots to decide whether or not their behaviour moves towards, or away from, their values, and the result is behaviour which either works, or doesn't work. Unfortunately, it has been my experience that many clients are overwhelmed by the perception that their life is mainly populated by things that don't work.

I often ask clients to imagine that they have before them a 'pile of stuff'. This pile of stuff represents them and their lives

---

4. Please note: There are some therapeutic settings and interventions which are *not* amenable to full and open disclosure. Some forensic and psychiatric circumstances require gradual exposure of information and a specific and predetermined set of therapeutic tools. Regardless of your setting and circumstances you do have an ethical right to engage in informed consent, even if you do not have the full process and tools made available to you at any one time.

completely, in other words 100 per cent of them. It contains their thoughts, memories, actions, beliefs, philosophies, morals, principles, ethics, words, failures and successes. This pile, in reality, contains only two types of things. Things that work, and things that don't work.

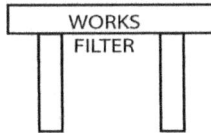

I invite them to imagine filtering off to their right all of the things that work. In this pile will be things that bring them joy, pride, satisfaction and that they would generally not need to change. I then ask them to move all of the things that don't work into a pile on their left. This pile contains things that incur feelings of shame, disappointment, anger or humiliation. These are things that they would prefer to change. I now ask them to determine what percentage of the original pile is now in each separate pile.

It is not uncommon for unhappy people to report that the pile of stuff that does not work greatly outweighs the pile that does work. People sometimes report a 50/50 split. And others report a higher value in the pile that works.

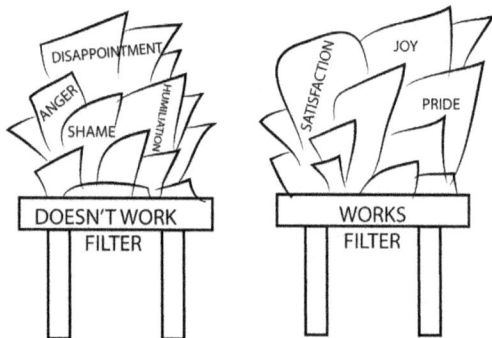

Regardless of the comparative sizes of your piles of stuff that work and don't work, most people would like the pile that works to be larger, and the pile that doesn't work to be smaller. This distance between where you are now and the place you would like to be is your reality gap. These reality gaps can be large or small, and may be present in various areas of your life.

A small reality gap might relate to a situation where I am sitting at home, bored, and I would like to go to a movie. If I have the money to go to a movie, if I can drive to the movie theatre, and if I can find a movie that would be reasonable and interesting for me, then my reality gap would be very small. So small reality gaps are ones where we don't have to work very hard, and we can close them rapidly.

A big reality gap might be if I decided that my life would not be meaningful unless I completed a marathon. As you get to know me further through this book, you will learn that I am not a particularly sporty person and that I am in my sixties. I will also let you know that marathon running has never been on my agenda in any way, shape or form. I've always found running to be fairly boring, really arduous, and I almost always end up experiencing some sort of muscle sprain or injury as a result of trying to run serious distances.

But let's imagine that I generated this legitimate and large reality gap, where running a marathon found its way onto my bucket list. If I was to go out this weekend and try to run a marathon, pay my fee, get all my gear for the support crew, and try to run forty-five or so kilometres, there is a 100 per cent chance that I wouldn't get more than a couple of kilometres.

This large reality gap would overwhelm my limitations. My lack of preparation, both psychologically and physically, would make this achievement totally unrealistic. This example of a large reality gap demonstrates how challenging big reality gaps can be.

Some common examples are losing weight and stopping smoking. In these instances, where people are trying to close a big reality gap, they have a reasonably clear vision of what they or their lives would be like at the other end of the process. They have a moderately clear vision of where they are right now, but the processes and procedures to fill in the gap are overwhelmingly complicated and challenging. The gap is too big to close.

What's interesting is that Auto Pilots aren't capable of closing these large reality gaps. Remember, your Auto Pilot is a machine of habit, so if you want to achieve something out of the ordinary, your Auto Pilot doesn't have the intelligence or initiative to do so. Instead, it will keep doing the things it has always done – the behaviours that it believes 'work'. And, because your Auto Pilot is in control most of the time, this can make it very challenging to overcome large reality gaps.

This is why your Clever Brain is required to close them.

Your Auto Pilot is an excellent doing machine, but it doesn't have the benefit of logic, foresight and an understanding of consequences. It automatically seeks out what it believes to be the quickest, easiest solution, which makes it the wrong brain to have in charge of closing a large reality gap.

If you reflect on the age-old sentiment, 'How do you eat an elephant?', the Auto Pilot approach is to take it all on at once.

As you know, though, the only way to eat an elephant is one bite at a time. The only way to close a large reality gap is to take small, strategic steps, one at a time. If I were to try and run a marathon then I would set out a plan and break down this goal into smaller chunks. I would give myself a minimum of a year to prepare for such an incredible thing, thereby giving myself a reasonable amount of time to close the reality gap. I would, in the first week, try to walk around the block half a dozen times. In the second week, I would try to jog around the block a few times. In the third week, I would attempt to run around the block a few times;

probably running and stopping and running and stopping. As the months of training unfolded, I would clock my performance, look at where I was meeting my goal's objectives, reflect on what was and wasn't working. And if I was dedicated enough and disciplined enough, hopefully, within a year – even at my advanced years – I would be able to struggle through a marathon.

It may take me over four hours to run it, but I would be able to cross that off of my bucket list.

A CLEVER BRAIN EXERCISE...

Evaluate your reality gap:

1. Divide a page into two columns. Write the heading 'Now' on the left column and 'Wow' on the right.

2. List where you are now in various areas in your life in the left-hand column, then describe your 'wow' scenario in the right-hand column.

3. Prioritise your reality gaps – start with the easiest and quickest, and finish with the largest and most challenging.

4. Identify any barriers to you closing your reality gaps and consider a meaningful timeline. Add steps and dates on the timeline and put the whole thing up on the wall where you will see it frequently.

5. Gradually and deliberately close the gap.

6. Once successful, move to the next easiest, then the next.

The 'pile of stuff' scenario

The 'pile of stuff' scenario, to which I referred earlier, is one way to get a general sense of your reality gap. In this exercise, clients imagine that the pile represents everything about them and their lives, and that this pile can be divided into two smaller piles – a pile of things that work, and a second pile of things that don't work.

For now; let's consider the things in your pile of stuff that don't work. We all have such a pile, and it contains things that are painful for us on some level. Imagine that you have just stepped on a nail and that it has pierced your shoe and stuck firmly into the bottom of your foot. What are you likely to pay attention to at that moment? The nail, of course! The fact that it is only affecting a tiny proportion of an otherwise pain-free body is of little consequence to you.

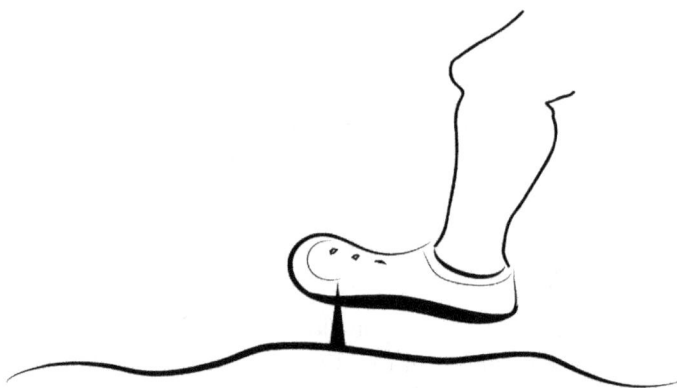

It would be ridiculous for you to then go to a psychologist and ask for pain management techniques so that your experience of the pain was reduced! You would, I hope, get the shoe off, get the nail out, and get the wound treated with antiseptic. This metaphor helps put the unworkable stuff into a more meaningful context. It allows you to determine the relative triviality of some of the stuff that doesn't work, and it also allows you to reflect on the actual size of the pile of stuff that does work.

However, generally only a few of the things that populate our 'doesn't work pile' can be removed and treated simply and by a third party. The majority of the psychological or environmental factors need to be fixed by *you*. This is the focus of this book – by changing the way you think (about how you think), you will have more power to fix these items.

The pile that doesn't work deserves further consideration and separation into two distinct piles – those things that you can fix, and those things you cannot.

If we consider the nail example again, a normal reaction to a nail in your foot would be to pull it out, clean the wound and apply a bandage, and pretty soon the pain will be a distant memory. The nail shows us that we can fix some of our stuff that doesn't work. Therefore one of the 'doesn't work' piles represents the things in our lives that we can rectify.

Examples of psychological stuff that falls into this pile include smoking, overeating, emotional arguing and road rage. These examples are all behaviours which do not work, negatively impact on our wellbeing, and are within our ability to control if we make ourselves aware of them before or as they are happening.

They also demonstrate that most unworkable behaviour carries with it some elements that kid us into thinking that they are working. Smoking is one example where smokers let their Auto Pilot selectively tell them that their habit works, and hide from them the parts that don't work. It is common to hear smokers report that they need a cigarette to relax. There is some truth in this statement – the rituals and habitual behaviours of smoking do have a calming effect on smokers. However, this calming effect is due to the countless number of times the smoker has had a cigarette in calm and relaxing circumstances, not due to the cigarette itself. These repeated experiences have trained their Auto Pilot to provide calm and relaxed emotions when a cigarette is being consumed. However, the physiological reality of a cigarette is that it is like a mini anxiety attack. Following a cigarette, your heart rate typically increases by around twenty beats per minute, alongside a host of other bodily reactions which mimic anxiety.

The second pile of stuff that doesn't work is the stuff that we cannot fix on our own. Extending the nail metaphor, imagine a pain that is chronic. Back pain, arthritis and bursitis are examples. Once again our Auto Pilot will constantly draw our attention to this unpleasant stimulus. So much so that the pain is often all we can focus on.

An example from my own life is age-related tinnitus, a constant ringing and hissing in my ears. My tinnitus began to make itself heard in my late forties and got progressively louder as the years went on. A referral to an ENT specialist informed me that, while it does have organic elements, tinnitus is a psychological problem. The ENT man told me that there have been examples where, in extreme cases, the medical profession has attempted to relieve roaring tinnitus by cutting the nerve which carries sound from the ears to the brain. He told me that such operations were carried out with humane intent, but that the outcomes were tragic. The patients were left profoundly deaf, except for their tinnitus! Psychological outcomes in such cases were, understandably, very poor. It is notable for me to report to you that, as I type this passage, my tinnitus is whistling and whispering very clearly and loudly in my ears. This is my experience every time I think about tinnitus. My usual experience of tinnitus is that I am not aware of it because I have trained my Auto Pilot not to bring it to my attention. Once my ENT specialist confirmed the chronic and untreatable nature of my tinnitus I realised, as a practicing psychologist, any resolution of the problem was up to me.

Following that definitive diagnosis I took responsibility for my Auto Pilot's habitual behaviours and trained it to pay auditory attention to other things in my life that did work for me. The reality is that I have played a trick on my Auto Pilot, and myself. The trick is that I do have chronic and untreatable age-related tinnitus, but I fool my Auto Pilot into not noticing it! It is important to note that I followed all reasonable avenues of formal medical treatment before I deliberately started to fool my Auto Pilot to ignore the symptoms of my tinnitus. It is not appropriate to ignore any physical symptoms until they have been thoroughly assessed, diagnosed and treated by medical doctors.

Focusing on the pile of stuff that doesn't work, and over which you have no power, is essentially a waste of time and energy. I struggle to imagine how anyone who was thinking with logic and clarity would spend time, energy and emotion on matters they were unable to resolve. I have the mixed blessing of being 175cm tall. I would prefer to be two metres tall because I know, psychologically, that people tend to instantly respect tall people and think about them in more positive ways than they do shorter people. However, without surgery or twenty-five-centimetre lifts in my shoes, I can do nothing about my height, and I perceive both of those alternatives to be fairly ridiculous. Rather than focusing on the fact that my height may not work for me, I take note of when it is on my mind (courtesy of my Auto Pilot) and I accept it, and mindfully refocus my thoughts on the many attributes of which I can be justifiably proud.

THE LUCKIEST MAN IN THE WORLD

It's important to keep in mind that we tend to over-report the pile of stuff that does not work. As discussed in the last chapter, this is because most of our life happens on Auto Pilot, and our Clever Brain only wakes up when something goes wrong. If our Clever Brain is only noticing what goes wrong, then of course we are going to give those elements of our lives more weight.

By contrast, there are many things that are 'working' for us on a daily basis that we take for granted. Consider your average day. You probably engage in thousands of behaviours, including getting dressed, eating breakfast, driving the car, talking, reading, working, and so on. If you really paid attention, what proportion of those behaviours work for you? It seems to me that, even in the most dysfunctional person, the proportion is going to be well above the eighty per cent mark. For most people it will be well above ninety per cent.

In the years that I have been walking the talk with this

approach my awareness of, and appreciation for, my pile of stuff that works has grown enormously. Without labouring the point I have found that focusing on the things that work enhances my enjoyment of my life overall. It brings the pile that works into comforting focus, it empowers me to influence the pile that doesn't work which I can influence, and it puts the other pile into a meaningful context and magnitude.

When it comes to closing your reality gap, reducing your 'Oh no!' moments and improving things in your pile of stuff that don't work might make life less miserable, but they do not necessarily make life more fulfilling. Paying attention to the multitude of 'Oh wow!' behaviours, emotions, reactions and experiences that populate the right-hand side of the Influence Diagram is what will lead you towards a rich, full and meaningful life. (More on 'Oh Wow' moments in *Chapter 6*)

The dividend that this focus has provided to me is that I regularly and honestly consider myself to be the luckiest man in the world. I say this in full knowledge that there are people whose lives may well eclipse mine, who may have better circumstances, and who may even be taller than me, but I still believe this to be true.

This philosophy can be summed up by an experience I had in my car on a bleak, rainy, windswept day in Melbourne. As I sat quietly in a gridlock, an inmate on day release from the nearby psychiatric institution walked through the traffic in front of my car. In a t-shirt, jeans and bare feet with lips nearly blue from cold he glanced into my car and we made accidental eye contact. I smiled and nodded to him and his face lit up with a beatific smile – it was like the sun coming out. I realised that a path to happiness is simply taking joy wherever you find it, even in the smile of a stranger on a cold and windy day. Needless to say, that man who blessed me with such a beautiful smile was surrounded by cars full of perfectly sane people who were also perfectly miserable.

A CLEVER BRAIN EXERCISE...

Write down or illustrate your own 'pile of stuff'. Draw two piles. The pile on the right contains all the stuff that works for you in life (things that bring you joy, pride, satisfaction – things that you don't need to change). The pile on the left represents all the things that aren't working for you (things that provide you shame, disappointment, anger, humiliation – things that you would like to change).

Look at and cherish the pile of stuff that does work. We often forget to dwell on and acknowledge the good in life – so please take time to get things in perspective and to remember that some things are pretty good.

Now to the pile of stuff that doesn't work. Separate this pile again into parts that are worthy and able to be changed and those things that are not worth fussing with or perhaps 'impossible' to change. I am hoping now that the pile of stuff that deserves your attention (the stuff in the 'not working' pile that is worthy and able to be changed) is much smaller than you first anticipated.

As you continue to work through this book, try to focus on what is working for you and also what you can and need to change. This change in focus will hopefully stop you from feeling overwhelmed and confused about how to go forward in life.

WHY CLEVER PEOPLE DO DUMB THINGS

Chapter summary

- Most of us are familiar with the process of 'benchmarking' and appreciate the benefits of being able to track progress. Likewise, knowing where you are and where you want to be are important markers in your journey of change.

- When you are reviewing your life, one helpful technique is imagining everything that encompasses your life is in a pile in front of you. In this 'pile of stuff' you will find things that work and things that don't.

- Many people feel overwhelmed as they think their life is mainly made up of stuff that doesn't work. This is because our Auto Pilot determines which parts of our environment get the most attention.

- The distance between where you are now and where you want to be is a reality gap. Large reality gaps cannot be solved by your Auto Pilot – you must involve your Clever Brain.

- The first step to feeling happier and at peace is focusing more on the things that work, and learning to redirect the things that don't.

GREAT
((CHANGE))
MAKER

WHY CLEVER PEOPLE
DO DUMB THINGS

CHAPTER 3:

ALIGN WITH YOUR VALUES

I have never met a person who regularly and deliberately sets out to incur speeding fines, yet I have met thousands of people who have incurred them – some to the point of losing their licences. This is clearly an example of clever people doing dumb things – often to the point of making their lives miserable.

Why? Because their Auto Pilot was left to solve an invisible dilemma. In this situation a person has two conflicting ideals. The first, and most conscious, is that you want to get to your destination as quickly as possible, and the second, and most invisible, is that you don't want to pay speeding fines. Your Auto Pilot is unable to weigh up the pros and cons of speeding, making him oblivious to this dilemma. This means he seeks immediate gratification over delayed and unlikely pain.

However, if detection was inevitable then you wouldn't speed because even your Auto Pilot would learn that the behaviour incurred more pain than pleasure. While there are some people who seek out pain as a means to pleasure, this book is not aimed at resolving psychiatric problems. If you are interested in this topic then you will need to read my next book *I can't talk at the moment – I'm all tied up!* [5]

---

5. Just a joke – my next book is not really about bondage and discipline!

The issue is that your Auto Pilot is unaware of values and your Clever Brain is off having a nap. As a result, your Auto Pilot makes habitual decisions that result in more 'Oh no!' moments and increasing the pile of stuff that doesn't work.

This means you need to train your Auto Pilot to habitually act in accordance with your values. However, before you can start training your Auto Pilot, you need to be aware of your values.

Important note: Recognising and accepting that your Auto Pilot is in control is an explanation of behaviour, not an excuse. Regardless of the stupid, dangerous, irresponsible or illegal behaviours controlling you, your Clever Brain must take full responsibility for your actions. There will always be 'Oh no!' moments after which your Clever Brain will need to clean up the mess. Keeping your Clever Brain awake will allow it to constantly influence your Auto Pilot and train it to act more in line with your values.

What are your values?

This seemingly innocent and simple question hides some really important and complex factors. The innocent part of the question usually elicits a response of 'I know what my values are'. Yet I have rarely met a person who has deliberately considered what their values might be.

The simple part of the question lies in the 'Oh no!' moments referred to throughout this book. These are the moments where our Clever Brain wakes up a little too late and realises that our Auto Pilot has just violated a value.

As I work with individual clients it often becomes clear that they have a strong sense of values in general but struggle with identifying what they might be and why they struggle with them on an everyday Auto Pilot level.

It is important to realise that your Auto Pilot does not know about, and does not care about, your values. It is also important to remind yourself (a lot!) that your Auto Pilot can only do what you have trained him to do. This is a potentially dangerous mix. As discussed in the Influence Diagram in *Chapter 1*, the Invisible Decision Point can lead us towards or away from our values. Because the Clever Brain is the place where logic, moral rectitude, problem solving, values and a sense of the consequences of our actions lives, if your Clever Brain is awake at this Invisible Decision Point, then the likelihood of your behaviour moving towards your values is increased. Likewise, training your Auto Pilot to do things that are in line with those values will also increase the likelihood of more workable behaviours.

As a result, developing a sense of what your values are is a worthwhile endeavour which, in my experience, very few people have actually done. This is a lifelong process which will increase the likelihood of you being a clever person who does clever things and who will be happier on the inside.

There is a range of ways to work out your values. They include:

- Considering what you admire about other people and adopting those traits. The famous story about George Washington, where he admitted to his father that he was the one who chopped down the apple tree and was forgiven because of his honesty, had a profound influence on my Auto Pilot. To this day I struggle to tell a lie and am uncomfortable with even omitting important truths. When I address this habitual behaviour with my Clever Brain I am aware that I do not want to change it as it is perfectly aligned with my values. Even if telling the truth gets me into trouble or offside with others.

- Considering what you do not like about others and embracing the opposite. I have had many clients who have had violent and alcoholic parents who have deliberately chosen temperance and non-violence. This kind of life experience clearly demonstrates our ability to recognise behaviour that does not align with our values and to be critical of that behaviour.

- Imagining that you are at your own significant birthday years from now. Surrounding you are all the people who have ever known you. Now imagine that each person is going to tell the gathering one thing about you. Which of those statements will you feel comfortable with everyone hearing, and which might make you cringe? You guessed it. The 'comfortable' things reflect your values and the 'cringe' ones are where you have acted contrary to your values. As you do this particular exercise don't beat yourself up too much over the 'cringe' examples. Remember that, until you read this book, your actions and words were generally selected for you by your Auto Pilot. (Remember, also, that this is an explanation of, not an excuse for, cringe-worthy behaviour!)

- A somewhat morbid but very effective way to consider your values is to picture your gravestone or epitaph. Is your current behaviour something that you would be happy to be remembered for? 'Here lies Lindsay, he lied to people' is not a behaviour for which I want to be remembered. 'Here lies Lindsay, he spoke the truth – even when it hurt' is an epitaph that I anticipate with some degree of comfort.

Here lies Lindsay –
he spoke the truth
even when it hurt

- Contemplating behaviour and habits that your children might reflect on should they need to talk to their own therapist one day can sometimes expose non-values-based behaviours. This is not a fool-proof technique as the role of a parent often requires one to act contrary to the Auto Pilot wishes of the child. Sometimes we accidentally raise narcissists and their memories and reflections will typically take note of hurts and frustrations to a greater degree than other more pleasant memories. However, it is still a worthwhile exercise to explore.

A CLEVER BRAIN EXERCISE...

Write down your true values in life. You will find a values worksheet on my website

www.greatchangemaker.com.au/CleverPeople

which may help you. Just formally identifying your values really helps you to focus on what is important and what is not. Because this may be difficult at first, start with the following:

- Think of people you admire – write down the traits they show, the way they go about life, the attitudes they portray, and so on.

- Think of traits and characteristics that you do not like. Whether these are things that you do or things other people do it doesn't really matter – what is important is that you identify the behaviours and attitudes and then go about trying to not exhibit them yourself.

- Write down how you think people might refer to you in a speech to celebrate your life. Or perhaps have a go at writing your own epitaph! This can be quite confronting and it is not meant to be an exercise in punishment. It is just designed to help you focus on what makes you comfortable and what doesn't. The speech or epitaph that makes you comfortable and happy is more than likely in line with your values. If, however, the exercise brings up aspects about your own behaviour that make you squirm, then it is a perfect opportunity for you to identify why.

- Consider, or even eavesdrop, what your children or other 'innocent' beings may say about you. Once again don't use this exercise as a punitive measure but use it as a fantastic opportunity to help you clarify your values and whether or not you are acting within them.

Once you've done these exercises, go through the list and decide whether there's anything missing.

Then on a scale of 1 to 10, with 1 being not at all and 10 being all the time, rate how well you think you strive and live by these values.

OUR VALUES HIERARCHY

One important aspect of values is that they do not exist on a level playing field. A famous psychologist named Abraham Maslow developed the Hierarchy of Needs where he identified that we have base needs which must be met before we can meet our higher needs. In its simplest form, this hierarchy describes that a person who is starving is unlikely to be able to cultivate social relationships until his hunger has been satisfied. Maslow powerfully argued that until our lower order needs are satisfied, we are unlikely to be able to pursue the higher order needs. For example, hunger is likely to outweigh the need to be loved. If we apply this hierarchy to our values we find that the reverse applies. That is, our higher-order values deserve our immediate attention, while the lower-order ones are more easily sacrificed. Unfortunately our Auto Pilot has no concept of values. It is equally comfortable in engaging in behaviours that are contrary to our values as it is in acting in accord with our values.

This can result in values dilemmas. A values dilemma is where there are two competing outcomes and both reflect your values. Using the example above, if my family is starving and my likeable neighbour has food but is unwilling to share, it is most likely that I will choose my family's survival and try to take the food (by force if necessary) rather than maintaining my value of keeping the relationship with my friendly neighbour and starving to death (such drastic behaviour might 'feel' better if my neighbour was a horrible person but the philosophy is the same). Thankfully most values dilemmas are not as extreme as this example. In this example Maslow is happy, I have addressed my lower order needs first, and my Clever Brain is happy, as I have met my higher order value.

Situations when you act contrary to certain values but when you are able to honestly acknowledge that your actions were justifiable, albeit difficult, are often a sign that you have sacrificed a lower-order value (hence the discomfort) to meet a higher-order value (hence the legitimate justification).

I recall my son's first serious asthma attack at around two years of age at 2am. Living in a relatively remote area, my wife and I elected to drive to the ER rather than wait for an ambulance to drive all the way out to our home. We also decided to exceed the speed limit in as prudent a manner as possible. Now neither of those decisions may have been particularly wise, but they were based on the value of caring for our son. Paradoxically, it has been one of my lifelong values to live my life within the law,

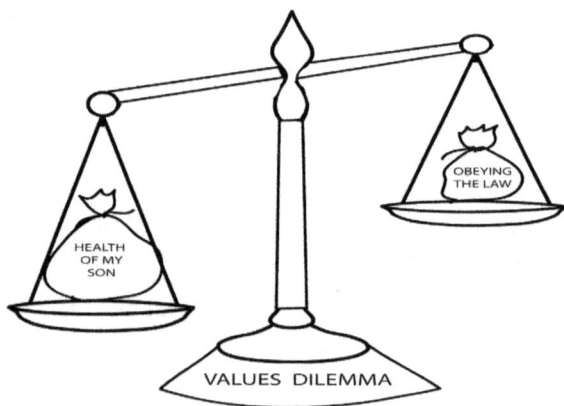

VALUES DILEMMA

yet here I was exceeding the speed limit deliberately and in full knowledge that, at times, my speed was excessive to the point that I might have lost my licence. I suspect that you can see where this is heading – I was willing to sacrifice my licence or some money for the wellbeing of my child.

As you can see, values are not all created equal. So how do you work out your values hierarchy?

The Two Boats Dilemma is a very deliberate way to consider the order in which your values might be rated. The Two Boats Dilemma invites you to imagine that you are standing on the banks of a rapidly flowing river. Just downstream from you is a waterfall, so great that anything falling over it will be destroyed. Floating along the river towards the waterfall are two boats. In each boat is one of your values. You have a rope in your hand and can only rescue one boat. The dilemma is to decide which boat you save. It is common for people confronted with this dilemma to try and generate novel ways to save both boats but that is contrary to the philosophical nature of the exercise. The idea of the Two Boats Dilemma is to bring your values hierarchy into sharp focus, not to generate guilt over which boat you sacrifice.

When I first became aware of the power of the Two Boats Dilemma I raised it in a conversation with my wife. When she requested an example I suggested that she consider that I was in one boat and our son was in the other – who would she choose? Without hesitation she said that she would throw the rope to our son and I was in immediate agreement. She then asked what I would do if she were in one boat, our son in the other, and I were on the shore with the rope. I answered without hesitation that I would save our son, to which she responded in mock seriousness, 'What about me?' In the conversation which followed we worked out that neither of us would be comfortable if we lived at the cost of our child's life. We had resolved a values dilemma. Now I sincerely hope that we never have to make that life and death decision, but it does show that values have different levels of importance, and that we can sort those levels out if we use our Clever Brain.

This fluid and dynamic aspect of values almost always means that our Auto Pilot is not qualified to resolve values dilemmas. If I had

A CLEVER BRAIN EXERCISE...

Consider some everyday values dilemmas:

- You notice a fellow employee stealing something from your employer and the material is your responsibility to safeguard. You know that the other employee will lose their job if you speak out, and the employee has already threatened you once when you commented on their behaviour.

- You discover pornographic images of children on the computer used by all members of your family, including your nineteen-year-old son. Your work requires you to have a police clearance, which you will lose if these images are discovered and you are blamed. However, you know that your son will suffer lifetime consequences if he is blamed.

If you are having difficulty contemplating these dilemmas then that is great! It means that your Clever Brain is trying to process the actions in a value-driven and intelligent way, rather than your Auto Pilot taking over.

Next, work through some value dilemmas based on your own values, either by yourself or with someone you trust. Find out what your sticking points are and find out what is at the base of them.

allowed my Auto Pilot to determine my driving behaviour on the night my little boy seemed to be gasping his last breath, then I almost certainly would have driven far more dangerously than I did and I may have compromised the value that I was trying to meet (the safety of my child) by putting him in danger by speeding through intersections, rather than just on straight sections of road. In that instance I was willing to compromise my values of obeying the law and not wasting money on speeding fines, but I was not willing to compromise my value of keeping my family safe.

It has been my observation that most problematic human behaviour can be traced back to the unhealthy resolution of values dilemmas. For example, people in abusive relationships are torn between their values of fidelity, loyalty, and providing an intact family for their children, and the values of personal security and being an effective role model for their children. The compromises that their Auto Pilot mindlessly requires of them commonly result in a further lowering of their self-esteem, an increase in their feelings of helplessness, and a potential increase in symptoms such as anxiety, which often make them more susceptible to further abuse.

So what's the solution? It comes down to reprogramming your Auto Pilot and awakening your Clever Brain.

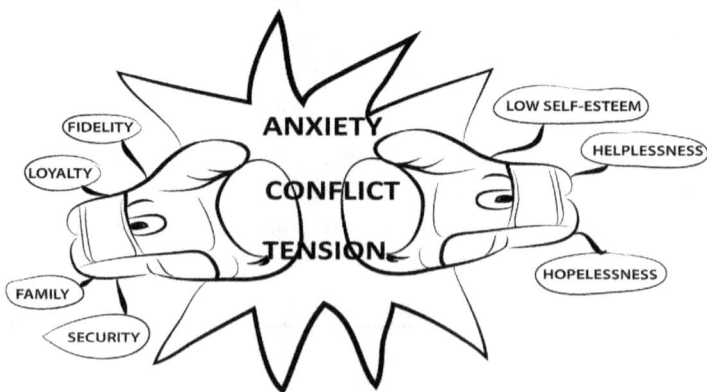

CHAPTER SUMMARY

- Values are essentially our attitudes, behaviours, and beliefs. They dictate how we feel about situations and they reside in our Clever Brain.

- Your Auto Pilot neither knows nor cares about your values and will not act in line with them unless you have trained him to do so.

- When we have an 'Oh no!' moment, it is because we have engaged in values-contrary behaviour. This moment is when our Clever Brain wakes up and realises what has happened.

- Some people find it difficult to identify their values, but there are some questions that can help.

- All values are not created equal – there is a hierarchy and you may sacrifice some values for others. Not being conscious of these can result in our Auto Pilot making the 'appropriate' decision in a split second, which can lead to issues as our Auto Pilot depends on accidental programming and emotional thinking. However, when our Clever Brain is awakened to resolve a values dilemma we have available to us the ability to use logic and to access our moral sense of values.

GREAT
((**CHANGE**))
MAKER

WHY CLEVER PEOPLE
DO DUMB THINGS

CHAPTER 4:

NUDGE YOUR AUTO PILOT

A recurring theme in this book is that your Auto Pilot is the brain which is capable of spontaneous and immediate reaction. Your Clever Brain is slower to act and almost completely unable to actually 'do' anything. This means that when you are presented with a situation which requires an instant resolution you typically, and invisibly, rely on your Auto Pilot to make the decision in a split second. Thankfully your Auto Pilot's decisions are based on habits, rules and opinions that it has learnt in a social and interpersonal environment. The Auto Pilot response is (hopefully) usually strongly aligned with your values.

These are the times when your Auto Pilot seamlessly resolves issues for you without you even noticing, and your behaviour moves to the right of the Influence Diagram. However, the resolution of these issues depends on accidental programming, and once your Auto Pilot has learnt these habits, rules, and opinions, it then applies them without regard or concern over whether or not they are logical, are morally right, resolve or create problems, fit with your values, or have unpleasant consequences. All of these aspects of our behaviour are the domain of our Clever Brain.

This means that relying on our Auto Pilot to resolve values dilemmas is fraught with danger. This is why there will certainly have been other times when your Auto Pilot has resolved these dilemmas in a way which is not in line with your values hierarchy, and where your behaviour moves to the left of the Influence Diagram. These can range from relatively trivial behaviours to highly dangerous or illegal behaviours. A commonly reported example from the trivial end of the scale is 'No darling, your bum doesn't look big in that dress'. This well-intentioned lie might meet the man's value of not hurting his wife's feelings, but the later consequences when she overhears another woman deriding her massive posterior will mean, at the very least, that her faith in his word will be eroded the next time she seeks his opinion. A sadly common example of values-contrary behaviour being determined by an Auto Pilot can be found in the ugly arguments that punctuate many intimate relationships.

Unfortunately, until now your Clever Brain has simply stood by and casually allowed your Auto Pilot to engage in this stupid, dangerous, irresponsible, unworkable, and values-contrary behaviour. Why? Because this Clever Brain is, in fact, a lazy brain which is capable of carrying out its job only when it is startled into wakefulness (which is usually after our Auto Pilot messes up, or when our environment provides feedback).

When you are driving on Auto Pilot and blue lights flash by the side of the road up ahead, your Reticular Activating System is the ever-alert part of your brain that wakes up your Clever Brain to determine if you are doing everything in line with the law and your values – if so, then it can go back to sleep. If not, it will go into damage control. If the damage is not able to be controlled, particularly over the long term, then the usual consequences are depression, anxiety, anger or stress. Our quality of life plunges, and we experience negative feedback from other people. This is often the time when people come to a psychologist for help.

Now consider what might happen if your Clever Brain was awakened to resolve these issues before you had an 'Oh no!' moment. You would have the ability to use logic, to access your moral sense of right and wrong, to use your capacity to solve problems, to refer to your values, and to use your foresight to consider the consequences of our actions. All of which can be done relatively unemotionally and outside of the limitations of your habitual behaviour.

To achieve this you will have to rely a little less on your existing, accidental programming and start intentionally programming your Auto Pilot to act in line with your values. This means you need to REANIMATE your Clever Brain so that its periods of awareness are more frequent and more deliberate so that it can train your Auto Pilot in those behaviours. Then, once your Auto Pilot has these new behaviours under control, your Clever Brain can again go off and sleep in the corner.

Case Study

One example of a client's experience with deliberately reprogramming their Auto Pilot is a young apprentice electrician who came to see me. Unfortunately it is not uncommon for apprentices to be bullied. In this instance, the young man's manager and co-workers were relentlessly critical of him. Now, as a first-year apprentice, you could imagine that he did not know much about the work that he was being exposed to, so there was plenty of opportunity for him to be criticised.

Our work together included focusing on the things that he brought to the job which were of value, and which legitimately deserved some positive observations. He was able to develop a list of his own attributes which made him feel good about himself. The list included that he was punctual, he was willing to learn, he was willing to accept that he made mistakes, and that he rarely made the same mistake twice. He was very good at his coursework and had a good theoretical understanding of the discipline in which he was getting his trade.

He also became more and more aware of the negative stories that his Auto Pilot was telling him. He began to realise that when he received criticism or harsh treatment, which was nothing short of bullying, his Auto Pilot was going along with the bullying. It would say, 'Well, you did make a mistake. You are pretty hopeless. You're going to take a long time to learn, your reality gap is enormous, you are living on the edge, and all of those people are so much smarter than you.'

But as our work progressed, he began to interrupt the flow of his automatic thoughts in a very deliberate way. And very tentatively, he reported to me that, on one occasion when his boss got very angry with him for not knowing how to do something, he actually said, 'I understand why you're angry at me for not knowing. In my perfect world, I would know everything. But do you think it is reasonable for a first-year apprentice to know what you just asked me?' And that questioning of the automatic negative attributions that the Auto Pilot had made was enough to get the boss's Clever Brain working.

In a few months, this young man was able to use that technique to turn around what was a very unpleasant workplace and almost single-handedly make it a far more positive and supportive workplace.

The role of your Clever Brain

Understanding the theory behind this model is very important. Understanding how to implement it in the real world can be a very different challenge. Beyond growing more comfortable with the idea that you might have two metaphorical brains, it is important to work out *how* to use those brains effectively.

As described earlier, I believe that the role of our Clever Brain is to be the manager, while our Auto Pilot is the employee.

Now, while our Clever Brain is lazy, it is also the place where logic, right from wrong, problem solving, values, and consequence evaluation lies, meaning it is a brain worthy of respect. At the time of writing there is a television program showing called *Undercover Boss*. In this show the CEO takes on a disguise and works at the coalface in their own company. In almost every episode that I have seen (yes, I am little bit addicted) the CEO makes a statement to a camera along the lines of, 'I could not do this job every day, it's too hard!' Now this always amuses me because the CEO is being paid many times what the line worker would be getting paid!

This example shows the divide between the Clever Brain and the Auto Pilot. The CEO is responsible for the executive functions of the company and the workers are responsible for making the company actually function at the grass roots.

However, as *Undercover Boss* frequently demonstrates, the CEO is often removed from reality, holding the belief that the organisation runs smoothly and according to policies and procedures. This illusion is based on the fact that the policies and procedures are carefully developed to ensure that the company's values and mission are being met. In Undercover Boss the CEO often sees examples of well-intentioned employees modifying procedures because they don't work, or developing procedures on the run because they have tried, without success, to get management to act. The CEO's reaction to such ad hoc behaviour is often disbelief and anger (or 'Oh no!' moments).

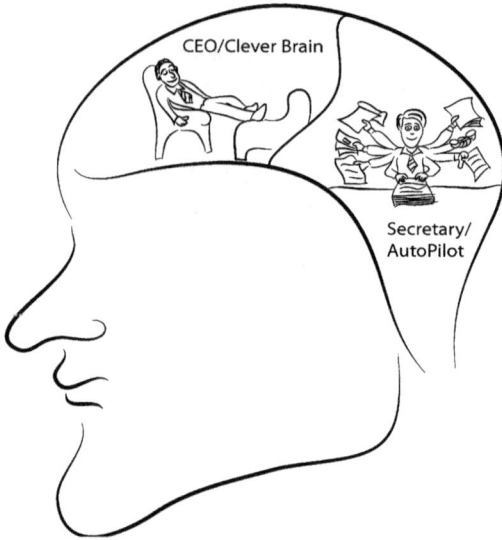

Until today, as a normal human being, your Clever Brain has been occupying the role of your CEO. This CEO has an incredibly efficient secretary which we are referring to as your Auto Pilot. This secretary's greatest desire is to avoid disturbing the CEO. She (forgive my stereotyping but I had to decide one way or the other) sits outside the CEO's office and runs interference without the CEO even noticing. She has worked for the CEO for his (oops – there is that stereotyping again!) entire life and she has an incredible ability to predict and meet his needs. She is so good at what she does that he no longer notices that she is doing almost everything for him. He has become accustomed to sitting in his corner office with his feet up on the desk, either snoozing or enjoying the view. Very occasionally she refers something to him for consideration and he makes a decision. He is content and secure in the belief that all is well. His comfort is sometimes disturbed by a crisis, but he quells the unease and deals with whatever has unsettled him, then he puts his feet back up on the desk. Unbeknown to him there is a fairly constant stream of people trying to get through to him to tell him that all is not well. These harbingers of doom are very efficiently dealt with by his secretary who either refuses them access to the CEO, or translates their messages into language that will not upset him. Sadly, she has never been trained in corporate management. She has no knowledge of balance sheets or breakeven calculations. She is completely ignorant of the need to generate profit. In other words, she neither knows nor cares whether the company is functional or dysfunctional – sound familiar?

CASE STUDY

In my early career I was a Sales Representative for a privately owned company which produced cheques (checks if you are in the USA) for commercial organisations. From my perspective, it was clearly a company in trouble. It produced a very high-quality product which had become commoditised by a competitive market. Its manufacturing base was rooted in a time when the company dominated the market and competitors were few. So while quality was very high, delivery times were chaotic and costs were out of control, leading to a shrinking customer base and increasing losses.

A new customer identified himself to me as a golfing buddy of our CEO and he clearly stated his high expectations regarding the order. He expected preferential treatment. He was outraged when I recommended that he seek an alternate proposal from a respected competitor. I did this because I was aware of the inevitable disappointment he would experience buying from our company. I knew that we were very expensive and very slow to deliver our high-quality product. He was insistent that I take his order and, sadly, equated our high price to his stated expectations of efficiency and reliability. When his job was delivered weeks later than our production team promised he exploded and insisted that I speak to the CEO regarding his dashed expectations.

I eventually stood before the CEO and owner of the company and related the sorry tale. His Auto Pilot reaction was an angry insistence that I identify those responsible for his embarrassment. When I indicated that I was in the presence of the guilty party (that is, the CEO himself) his Auto Pilot provided even more outrage.

To his credit, he finally calmed down and we had a Clever Brain conversation about how remote he had become from the operations of the company. It was moving to observe him recall earlier days when he knew every employee by name and the company was both functional and profitable. At the time of this discussion I had been with the company for two years and we had not only never met, but he had never even visited the building where I worked. All this in a company employing fewer than 200 people with only five operating sites. His Clever Brain had fallen asleep in the halcyon days when cheques were highly specialised documents and there were few competitors. His lazy Clever Brain had been lulled into a sense of complacency and his Auto Pilot (direct reports such as line managers and his secretary) had run the company into the ground. Sadly, this company closed down a few months later.

Please don't think that I am advocating that you start getting your Clever Brain to carry out front-line activities. The role of management is not to be at the coal face doing the hard work. It is not qualified to do so and will interfere with your efficiency if you do. *Undercover Boss* clearly shows how incompetent the CEO can be at delivering front-line services. Like a successful CEO in the real world, your Clever Brain's job is to manage and supervise, to guide and direct, and to ensure that your organisation is running efficiently from an overall perspective. But a CEO who sits in their ivory tower and allows the entire organisation to be run on Auto Pilot runs the very real risk that their organisation will run itself to ruin.

Currently your Auto Pilot is acting without conscious management. That means it is your Auto Pilot alone who determines whether your behaviour moves you towards, or away from, your values.

So who's managing your Auto Pilot?

Interestingly, your Auto Pilot is already acting in a way that is in line with your values most of the time. In fact, in *Chapter 2*, I estimated that the proportion of values-based or workable behaviours would be above ninety per cent for most people. Can you imagine how successful an organisation would be if all of its employees were effective over ninety per cent of the time? Especially when those employees worked twenty-four hours a day, seven days a week, and were willing to do so for free and without recognition or reward of any kind! These considerations led to me developing a deep appreciation and respect for my Auto Pilot. 'Buddy'[6] is my greatest ally and closest associate – it's not his fault that he is deaf, mute, blind and stupid!

To date, your Auto Pilot hasn't been given any conscious management, and has developed his behaviours by accident. And, being deaf, mute, blind and stupid, he doesn't have the resources to question any of these behaviours. Fortunately, this is moderated by the fact that we usually take on feedback from our environment. However, while this can be valuable, and is the reason why ninety per cent of your behaviours 'work', the issue is that this feedback is limited to our perceptual funnel.

We humans have, by necessity, a superb filter to reduce the number of things we pay attention to. If we did not have this brilliant device then we would very quickly be overwhelmed and paralysed by the environmental triggers to which we are exposed. The result of this perceptual filter is that we tend to see the world as if looking through a funnel. The younger we

6. It has been my experience that giving your Auto Pilot a name makes talking to him a lot easier. I have observed that many of my clients come up with clever and appropriate names for their Auto Pilot. Some initially come up with very uncomplimentary and judgemental names but, after a conversation regarding the inherent usefulness and innocence of their Auto Pilot, they usually find a name that is more in keeping with their values and their Auto Pilot's general usefulness. Just for the record, my Auto Pilot's name is 'Buddy', as he is my loyal friend and he is always with me.

are and the fewer experiences we have, the more limiting, or narrow, the funnel. As we age and gain knowledge, experience and wisdom, the wider our funnel becomes. (One of my favourite bumper stickers reads, 'I'd rather be an old fart than a young fool'.) Unfortunately our funnel is still a funnel and new information which is too far outside our funnel will be incomprehensible or ignored.

When it comes to our Auto Pilot, if the feedback from our environment is outside our funnel then we will probably *not* hear it or understand it – and our Auto Pilot will carry on creating unworkable behaviours. It will keep doing this even if the outcome is contrary to our values! We will only realise that our values have been compromised when our Clever Brain wakes up and we have an 'Oh no!' moment, and that is almost always just that little bit too late.

Consider people who are overweight. They are constantly being given 'advice', and they are constantly ignoring it. These people are often judged as being 'lazy' or 'making bad choices'. But a quick review of our environment discloses that we are all subject to relentless advertising messages to eat more sugary, fatty, processed, calorie-laden food. Obese people potentially have their perceptual funnel focused on the messages that their Auto Pilot is habitually attracted to, rather than what their values might reflect. Fatty and sugary fast food is marketed as easy, cheap, delicious and fun. All true! All attractive to our Auto Pilot! Only our Clever Brain can fill in the missing information that it is fattening, unhealthy, and that we are being manipulated by clever marketers.

Because our perceptual funnel is limited, our environment can only train our Auto Pilot to a certain extent. So what we end up with is an incredibly enthusiastic but incredibly stupid employee, who is very capable of being trained, but who is not capable of training himself, and this results in habitual 'Oh no!' moments.

It became clear to me that if I was to manage such a motivated but challenged employee, I would need to take true responsibility for his actions. 'Buddy' is, after all, delivering all of my behaviour and actions – he provides my emotional responses, he populates my personality, and he monitors and maintains my bodily functions. Can you imagine owning a business which employed someone with such responsibility and not carefully overseeing them, measuring their performance and nurturing them as if your life depended on it?

This is where our Clever Brain comes in. Our Clever Brain's role is to train and manage our Auto Pilot, or reprogram him with an increasingly complex set of rules. In the world of computer programming, this might be called an algorithm or a 'Yes/No' diagram. We establish a series of 'If this happens, then do that, else do something different' statements, and we develop habitual responses accordingly. In scenarios where the 'Yes/No' diagram is incomplete, our Auto Pilot will seek instant gratification (fast food = yum!). This decision will be fleetingly okay, but we may well regret it when our Clever Brain notices that we don't fit into our jeans anymore!

So how do you do it?

You are already halfway through the journey. You have recognised that you are not in control, you have evaluated your reality gap, you have aligned with your values and you have started to nudge your Auto Pilot. Over the coming chapters, you will learn how to influence your Clever Brain, actively manage your Auto Pilot, use these practices in your everyday life and empower others to positively influence your Auto Pilot.

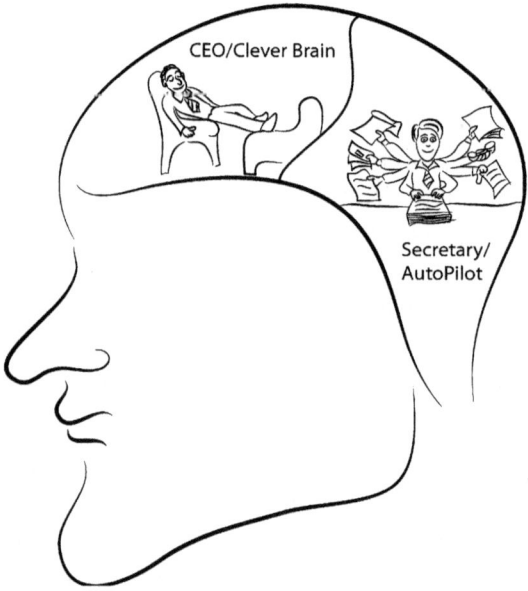

Chapter summary

- Our Auto Pilot is the brain which is capable of spontaneous and immediate reaction, while our Clever Brain is slower to act and almost completely unable to actually 'do' anything.

- A helpful analogy is imagining your Clever Brain occupying the role of CEO, and your Auto Pilot in the role of secretary. This secretary's greatest desire is to avoid disturbing the CEO. Occasionally the secretary may need to refer something to the CEO so he can make an important decision, but otherwise the secretary virtually runs the show.

- Despite attempts by people to access the CEO, the secretary often blocks access and makes many decisions she is not qualified to make. It is inevitable that the 'corporation' under such a management system will get into trouble.

- While challenged, this secretary, your Auto Pilot, is very trainable. However, to date, your Auto Pilot hasn't been consciously trained. Instead, he has been trained by accident based on feedback from your environment, which moderates and adjusts your behaviour.

- Because we each have a limited perceptual funnel, sometimes we are unable to take on this feedback and we continue to act in a way that is not helpful and is contrary to our values.

- This is why we need to reprogram our Auto Pilot.

GREAT
((CHANGE))
MAKER

WHY CLEVER PEOPLE
DO DUMB THINGS

CHAPTER 5:

INFLUENCE YOUR CLEVER BRAIN

One of the underlying beliefs in this book is that you have become the person you are by chance. Your Auto Pilot has been gradually programmed by your environment over your entire life. Most of that programming works, but enough of it doesn't work for you to have been motivated to read this far into this book. Having come this far, then, I think it is safe to assume that you would prefer to make some changes to your Auto Pilot's programming.

As you know, your Auto Pilot neither knows, nor cares, now whether its behaviour is in line with your values. In the early stages of my work with clients I often ask them to reflect on whether they have a 'feeling' regarding their behaviour. The classic psychological term for this is 'cognitive dissonance', that instant where you know something is wrong without actually being able to identify what it might be. It is my opinion that cognitive dissonance is your Clever Brain beginning to wake up and realising that your Auto Pilot is processing something in a manner contrary to your values.

As an example, many obese people describe the feeling of guilt when they eat in excess. It is reasonable to imagine that if they actively thought about and processed the consumption of the food with their Clever Brain prior to eating it, they may begin to deliberately influence their eating in a more positive way.

This proactive thought process diminishes their Auto Pilot's control of their actions, helps them assume responsibility in the moment, and increases the likelihood of their Clever Brain influencing their behaviour. Sadly, our Auto Pilot comes with some hard-wired programming. Anxiety is an obvious one, but overeating is one seldom considered. If you subscribe to the Darwinian explanation of how we got here then it will seem obvious that those ancestors who survived famines did so by gorging on food when it was available, and having a tendency to eat calorie-rich food in order to store fat to survive famines. This aspect of evolutionary programming belies some of the blame that obese people feel and receive due to their eating habits. Luckily, even such pre-programmed behaviour is amenable to Clever Brain intervention.

So how can your Clever Brain intervene? We need to return to the Influence Diagram.

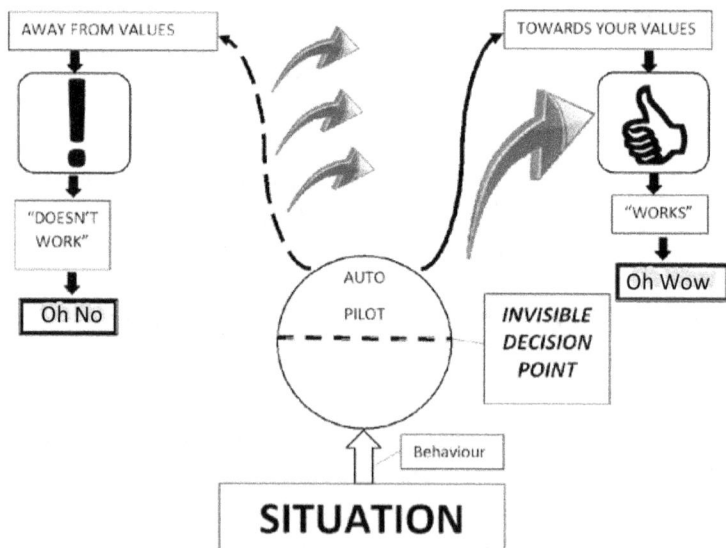

As discussed in *Chapter 1*, there is an Invisible Decision Point where our Auto Pilot chooses how it will respond to a situation. This is when it would be nice to think that we have control over our behaviour; however, because our Auto Pilot is running the show we rarely make these decisions with intent. When our Auto Pilot innocently compromises our values, this leads to 'Oh no!' moments when our Clever Brain wakes up, usually too late in the process.

I can recall a time when my Clever Brain activated just a little too late in an ugly domestic argument early in my current incredibly fulfilling relationship. I have no idea what the cause of the argument might have been (it is twenty-four years ago at the time of writing this book) but I do recall that I 'won' the argument through sheer force of personality and volume. I stormed out of the room filled with self-righteous bluster and slammed the door behind me. I now know that the slamming of the door activated my Clever Brain. At the time all I realised was that I came to standstill in the hallway and became aware of the sobs of my partner from the room I had just left.

I recall as if it were yesterday the voice in my mind asking, 'How could you do that to the woman you love?' It was simple – my Auto Pilot was faced with the conflict between my desire to prove myself right (even if I wasn't!) and my desire to maintain a loving and harmonious relationship with the person I loved. (This relates to the discussion in *Chapter 3 – Align with your values*. I just didn't realise it at the time!)

Once my Clever Brain kicked in I was able to deliberately act on my values and went back into the room to heal the wound. I was then able to develop, Clever Brain to Clever Brain with my now wife of over twenty years, rules of engagement which have given us a rich and relatively harmonious life together. A year or so ago our son, then around eleven years old, asked us over breakfast why we never argued. We determined that, while he had observed disagreements between us, he had also recently observed a fairly active and emotionally charged disagreement at a friend's house. He reported loud voices, swearing, walls being punched and dishes thrown. It had impacted on him to the point where he had been processing it for some weeks before he raised it with us over breakfast. I finally asked him why he thought his mother and I could disagree without resorting to argument and his response made twenty-five years of study, professional development, and hard work all worthwhile. He said 'Is it because you use your Clever Brains when you disagree?'

I cite this example because it demonstrates the capacity of our Clever Brain to make long-term changes in the programming of our Auto Pilot to ensure that our values can be met in the future.

While an argument is an extreme example, you can also use your Clever Brain to review and reprogram more subtle behaviours that aren't in line with your values.

You should already have some idea of these – you've looked at what is and isn't working in your life, and you've also clarified your values, which indicate which of your behaviours are to the left or right of the Influence Diagram. Now it's time to identify specific behaviours, as well as the common situations that trigger them.

These situations are when you need to start using your Clever Brain.

A CLEVER BRAIN EXERCISE...

To build upon the identification of your values I want you to consider situations where (or when) these values are compromised.

Grab a few copies of the Influence Diagram[7] and start plotting the process and outcomes of these situations. Plot both the 'Oh wow!' ones and the 'Oh no!' ones. Complete all parts of the diagram and use it to gather insights in to how situations are created.

To work through an example let's consider my history as a speeding driver. The situation at the bottom of the diagram would be the need to get from Point A to Point B. The behaviour that typically emerged from that behaviour was influenced by my Auto Pilot, without my conscious thought, and led me to exceed the speed limit. This behaviour persisted even when I was manually detected and fined. My Auto Pilot had learnt to defend its own behaviour with seductively rationalising thoughts such as 'This is my speeding tax' and 'I am as safe at 75kph as everyone else is at 60kph. (Please note that I have already acknowledged the inherent stupidity in these rationalisations). The speeding behaviour clearly moves to the left side of the diagram as my strong social value is to be a law abiding citizen. Unfortunately my behaviour endured until the advent of automated detection devices increased the impact and frequency of my 'Oh No!' moments and I prevailed upon my Auto Pilot to learn new habits related to the speed at which I drove.

It is really useful to analyse what happened in the 'Oh no!' scenario as it will identify your conflicting values. In these circumstances, try to list the values you were trying to achieve and the value you actually employed. If you do this you will probably notice that not all values are created equal, as discussed in *Chapter 3*.

Of course this analysis is not always practical when you are in the middle of a situation, but doing it in retrospect can help you identify common patterns, while doing it immediately after the event it will provide you with great learning that you can use to reprogram the interactions between your dumb Auto Pilot and your Clever Brain

---

7. Visit my website to download free copies.
   www.greatchangemaker.com.au/CleverPeople

Mindful, mind full or mindless?

While awareness of the common unworkable behaviours of your Auto Pilot and the situations that trigger them is important, to actually change those behaviours you need to make a deliberate commitment to assume responsibility for his actions as *they unfold*. By waking your Clever Brain, you can interrupt your Auto Pilot's actions *before* you have an 'Oh no!' moment, and you can then direct your actions towards your values and have more 'Oh wow!' moments.

In my case, imagine what might have happened all those years ago in that argument if I had been able to activate my Clever Brain earlier. Rather than allowing my Auto Pilot to decide that anger, defensiveness, and volume were appropriate, I would have been far more likely to actually listen, to ensure that I was heard, and to have resolved the disagreement in a manner that was in line with my values.

So how can you activate your Clever Brain earlier? With mindfulness.

Mindfulness has become a very popular, hackneyed and misunderstood term. With the emergence of ACT, Positive Psychology, neuroplasticity and a range of other fantastic interventions, there has emerged an alarming tendency for therapists and self-help gurus to embrace some aspects of mindfulness as a form of easy therapy. For example, there is growing evidence that meditation is a psychologically beneficial activity. Sadly I have heard a number of examples where therapists, hopefully with good intent, use recorded, generic visualisations to facilitate the relaxed and empty mind commonly associated with mindfulness. I suspect that much of this behaviour is an unintentional application of 'mindlessness' which, while providing some temporary relief from the vicissitudes of life, is a relatively passive approach to therapy.[8]

---

8. That said, 'mindlessness' is preferable to the 'mind fullness' which represents the mental state of many people presenting for therapy. In this state of mind the person is under the control of whatever their Auto Pilot presents to them in the way of memories, thoughts, emotions and reactions. That's fine if it is stuff that works, but very few people present for therapy citing behaviours and reactions that work as the reason they are seeking help.

The REANIMATE process is designed to encourage true and active mindfulness. Rather than simply emptying the mind, the aspect of meditation which resonates with ACT is emptying the mind in favour of experiencing the present moment. In the terminology used in this book, 'mindfulness' might be described as the deliberate activation of the Clever Brain to quieten the useless chatter of the Auto Pilot and allow us to move towards our values.

Guided mindfulness recordings can provide significant shifts in Auto Pilot behaviour. They facilitate neuroplasticity and thereby generate more functional neural pathways leading to beneficial psychological outcomes.

How? Mindfulness allows your Clever Brain to observe the behaviour of your Auto Pilot and influence whether or not you engage in activities, behaviours, actions and words which are in line with your values. This is far preferable to a life where your Auto Pilot makes these choices and you only get to know about them after the event, when it is too late to do anything other than go into damage control.

MINDFULNESS EXPLORED

The practical way to experience mindfulness is to develop the routine of checking what your Auto Pilot is doing, of taking notice of when he is acting in accord with your values, and of deliberately modifying his actions when he is moving you away from your values.

One technique I've found to be very valuable for awakening my Clever Brain to influence my behaviour is a relaxation trick I learnt to rapidly reduce anxiety. This technique was so effective for me that I have taught it to clients in my private practice with great success for many years. When I first learnt this technique it was presented as Pavlovian, or Classical, Conditioning. Ivan Pavlov was a Russian scientist who discovered that if food is presented to a dog at the same time as another stimulus, say a bell ringing, the dog will soon associate the bell with food and will ultimately salivate when the bell is rung in the absence of food. In the context of the two brain metaphor, you can use your Clever Brain to train your Auto Pilot to invoke a relaxed state using a trigger which would not normally produce a relaxed state. In my case, I taught my Auto Pilot when I touched my thumb to my middle finger I would be relaxed and calm. It soon obeyed me and I became relaxed and calm using this trigger.

When it comes to awakening your Clever Brain, using a simple relaxation trigger like this is one way to become mindful in the heat of a situation. My first use of this relaxation trigger was during a trivial but nasty argument with a work colleague. He had, with some justification, objected to my having taken and used his stapler without permission. I had done so in the unstated belief that the stapler was company property and therefore not his property. The resulting argument was becoming heated to the point where I suddenly realised that I was becoming upset and anxious. I had my hand in my pocket and, unknown to him, I touched my thumb to my middle finger and mentally stated that I was calm and relaxed. The immediate effect was that my level of anxiety dropped radically and produced a feeling of mild euphoria. His reaction to the involuntary smile on my face was an immediate escalation of his irritation to the point of anger and he, somewhat harshly, demanded to know what I found so amusing.

I now know that the trigger had awoken my unemotional and logical Clever Brain. I was now able to access my values and problem solving abilities and consider the consequences of my actions. I immediately acknowledged that my actions were inappropriate, apologised for the distress I had so clearly caused, and went about resolving the tension by obtaining a brand new stapler which I gave to him in exchange for his used, but perfectly functional, stapler. The end result was that he and I became firm friends for the remainder of our time working together. This technique interrupted the flow of my Auto Pilot away from an 'Oh no!' moment and diverted him towards an 'Oh wow!' moment.

It is worth noting that, while our Auto Pilot is really good at learning habits, he rarely does so deliberately. My use of this anxiety reducing trigger was made possible by my deliberately training my Auto Pilot over a period of weeks. By mindfully alerting my Clever Brain to many moments when I was at a very low level of anxiety, and deliberately bringing my thumb to my middle finger and thinking consciously that I was calm and relaxed, I trained my Auto Pilot in a new habit, one of feeling calm and relaxed when I touched my thumb to my middle finger.

Fortunately you already have awareness of the common situations that lead to unworkable, automatic behaviours, which means you know some of the situations that require your Clever Brain to be more vigilant. These are situations where you can practise waking your Clever Brain in the moment, which will make it easier for you to wake this brain when unexpected situations arise.

A CLEVER BRAIN EXERCISE…

Experiment with using a relaxation trigger to help train your Auto Pilot to act in a calm manner. To get started, try practicing my relaxation trigger of touching your middle finger with your thumb whenever you find yourself in a calm, relaxed and happy state. After a few weeks of mindfully doing this when things are going well for you, then try it when you are experiencing a less-attractive emotion such as anger, sadness, anxiety or frustration. In time, you will find that you automatically become more relaxed which, in turn, will lead to less emotional responses and decisions.

Keep in mind that if you decide to try to teach your own Auto Pilot this habit then there are pretty much only two things that will stop it working. One is if you don't practice enough – this is an exercise which you cannot over practice, but you can definitely under practice. The second way to make it fail is if, having learnt it, you then fail to use it – this will prevent your Auto Pilot from making it a habit.

This isn't always as easy as it sounds. Developing mindfulness requires awareness and intent in the early stages of the self-change process. It is seductively easy to lapse back into surrendering control of your life to your Auto Pilot. He will love you for it as it is what he does. You probably won't notice until you have an 'Oh no!' moment. Each of these lapses is a just-too-late reminder that your Clever Brain has fallen asleep (don't forget that it is lazy) and you have been under the thrall of your enthusiastic, but dumb, Auto Pilot. Fortunately, the more you do this, the easier it gets, and the more your Clever Brain demonstrates appropriate behaviours, the faster your Auto Pilot will learn to replicate those behaviours automatically.

In the end, this practice of mindfulness will allow you to reduce the number of 'Oh no!' moments in your life.

MAKING DECISIONS, MINDFULLY

Making difficult decisions seems to be the bane of mankind. Do I stay with my partner or leave? Do we have kids or not? Should I take that new job? Do we buy the house with the big block on the busy road or the one with the pool in the cul-de-sac?

Most people seem to try to resolve the difficult questions in life by thinking about them, talking about them, or asking other people for their opinion. All of these approaches are incredibly normal, but they leave you prey to the influence of your Auto Pilot, and other people's Auto Pilots.

However, if you make those decisions *mindfully*, this will awaken your Clever Brain, meaning that not only do your day-to-day behaviours become more intentional, but so do your big decisions.

One of the most powerful tools to achieve this is a Decision Matrix, a tool I discovered early in my career as a psychologist when I focused on organisational psychology. The Decision Matrix works on the understanding that any decision requires the comparison of at least two competing ideas, usually to the mutual exclusion of each other. It also recognises that, for a dilemma to exist, each idea must have costs and benefits.

These four aspects are represented in a matrix as follows:

	Option One	?/10	Option Two	?/10
FOR	Consideration A	6	Consideration A	3
	Consideration B	7	Consideration B	10
	Consideration C	5		
	Consideration D	10		
		28		13
AGAINST	Consideration A	6	Consideration A	4
	Consideration B	3	Consideration B	7
			Consideration C	9
			Consideration D	8
			Consideration E	7
		9		35

Creating a Decision Matrix is fairly simple:

1. Decide what the two (or more) options are and put them at the top. I have shown them as Option One and Option Two.

2. Consider each aspect of the Matrix independently (this is the challenging bit). Write down every argument or consideration, regardless of how you feel regarding each consideration.

3. Review all of the considerations to determine whether any of them are 'Deal Breakers' or 'Deal Makers'. In other words, do any of the considerations overwhelmingly influence

the decision? If you find a Deal Maker or a Deal Breaker, then your work is done. There is no point putting any more effort into the Matrix. If there are conflicting Deal Makers or Breakers, or none of either, then keep working.

4. Having exhausted all of the considerations, and determined the absence or conflict of Deal Makers or Breakers, you then quantify each of the considerations. In the column marked '?/10', evaluate the importance of each consideration on a scale of 1 to 10. A score of 1 indicates a trivial consideration. A score of 10 indicates a very strong consideration.

5. Having evaluated each consideration numerically, add up the total of each quadrant and see what the numbers tell you.

6. The most common outcome of a Decision Matrix exercise is that the 'For' and 'Against' totals show a diagonal trend and therefore indicate the inevitable decision. In the example shown above the totals for Option One and against Option Two are overwhelmingly higher than the total for Option Two and against Option One. In this example, the Clever Brain outcome would be to go with Option One.

If the diagonal trend is not apparent, that is the four totals are very close to one another, and there are no Deal Makers or Deal Breakers, then the decision is a genuine dilemma and requires outside influence. My opinion is that such a 'tied' dilemma deserves to be set aside for a week or so, and then reviewed. If still tied, then the toss of a coin is the only sensible way to avoid being eternally stuck. Given that the alternative is to remain torn between the equally attractive or repulsive alternatives, making an arbitrary decision is the only way out.

My first personal use of this tool was during a very difficult time in my life. We were struggling financially but were still living in our dream home. Our financial meltdown had resulted in us having a huge mortgage which was sending us broke. We were going backwards with a growing mountain of debt but were too emotionally attached to our house to sell it. Eventually it occurred to me to put all of the considerations into a Decision Matrix. It took a few days to get everything down. The result was resoundingly in favour of us downsizing. I then asked my wife to do the exercise and her results mirrored mine, but with many differing arguments. We introduced the idea to our then nine-year-old son and, again with very different arguments, he produced an identical result. Merging the three matrices proved to us that we had no logical option but to sell our beautiful home and buy a much cheaper one. The resultant journey was highly emotional but eventually resulted in us living in the beautiful 105-year-old grand Queenslander that we have grown to love, in an area which has proved to be more liveable for us in ways that we could never have imagined.

Using a tool such as the Decision Matrix allows both brains to have input into the decision, but to allow the decision to be made according to Clever Brain principles. Such a decision will often involve emotional cost, but that is what usually freezes people when they are in the grip of a dilemma.

A CLEVER BRAIN EXERCISE...

You guessed it – I suggest you start using a Decision Matrix every time you find yourself experiencing major indecision. While we don't have the time to do a Decision Matrix on the run, it is still a very useful tool, even if you do it retrospectively.

CHAPTER SUMMARY

- Your Auto Pilot neither knows, nor cares, whether its behaviour is in line with your values. However, often you will have a 'feeling' regarding their behaviour and know something is wrong without knowing what it might be. This is your Clever Brain beginning to wake up to values-contrary behaviour.

- Instead, you want your Clever Brain to both reflect on past values-contrary behaviours so you can avoid them in future, as well as learning to intervene at the Invisible Decision Point before those 'Oh no!' moments occur.

- The key to awakening your Clever Brain at the Invisible Decision Point is to invoke a relaxed state during any situation that might arouse unworkable behaviours. To do this you need to develop a trigger that you can use in difficult situations. In time you will be able to awaken your Clever Brain proactively.

- It is also important to activate your Clever Brain when making important decisions. A Decision Matrix is one useful way to do this.

CHAPTER 6:

MANAGE YOUR AUTO PILOT

Beyond using your Clever Brain to choose values-based behaviours, you want to train your Auto Pilot to take over these workable behaviours and make them automatic. To do this, you need to actively manage your Auto Pilot.

Unfortunately, as we've discussed, most Auto Pilots suffer from poor management. What do I mean by poor management? If the job of a manager is to reinforce positive behaviour, correct negative behaviour and set an overall good example, then this is what your Clever Brain should be doing. If your Clever Brain isn't doing these things, that is a case of poor management.

Positive reinforcement

It is my belief that when our Auto Pilot arbitrarily chooses to take our behaviour in the direction of our values, we tend *not* to notice it. However, if our Clever Brain is actively engaged in supervising our Auto Pilot, it then has the opportunity to notice when our Auto Pilot gets it right!

Now we have the potential to begin to mindfully explore all of those things in which we can take real and genuine pleasure. Hitting that tennis ball back over the net to just the place you wanted it, typing that letter without an error, or proactively marshalling the required resources to comfortably meet a work deadline. All of these examples live in the pile of stuff that works.

Why is this important? It comes back to the idea of the Clever Brain being the manager, or CEO, and the Auto Pilot being an employee. During my long working life I have found myself, at those times I could not avoid it, having to employ and manage other people. When this happened in my early twenties I was a horrible boss. I was inflexible, opinionated, demanding and generally unpopular. None of these attributes reflected my values and I was, of course, on Auto Pilot. As a manager in my forties and fifties I was popular and relatively successful because I had finally realised that people in general are well-intentioned. If you give staff the chance to shine, and catch them doing it, you will have a generally happy and highly functional team. I had finally awakened my Clever Brain enough to modify my accidental program and begin to act in accordance with my values.

However, my observation of managers in general is that they see their job as policing, or seeking out their staff doing things wrong. As a psychologist, I've found the basic flaw in the policing approach is that if you pay attention to any particular behaviour, then you tend to perpetuate that behaviour.

Taking delight in the behaviours which work is legitimate. Positive feedback, from a behavioural perspective, is likely to increase the frequency of those behaviours. As shown as shown on next page, it leads to a life where there are fewer 'Oh no!' moments, and many more 'Oh wow!' moments.

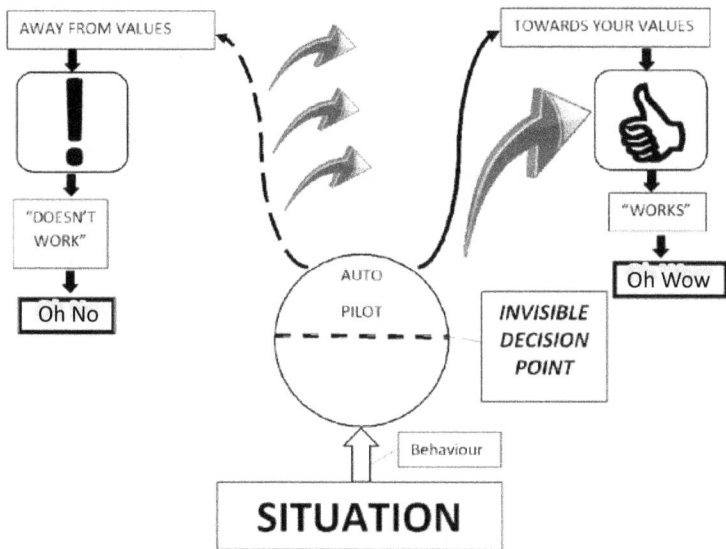

```
AWAY FROM VALUES                           TOWARDS YOUR VALUES

    ┌─┐                                          👍
    │!│
    └─┘
  "DOESN'T                                     "WORKS"
   WORK"
                        AUTO                    Oh Wow
  Oh No                 PILOT        INVISIBLE
                                     DECISION
                                      POINT

                              Behaviour
                   SITUATION
```

A
CLEVER BRAIN
EXERCISE...

Return to your list from *Chapter 2* of the things that are currently working for you and the things that aren't. I hope you may be surprised by the number of things that you are getting right. Give yourself and your Auto Pilot a pat on the back.

Try to make it a habit to pay attention to what your Auto Pilot is doing. Catch him doing the good things as well as the less helpful things. Redirect him when necessary but, most importantly, praise your Auto Pilot for all of the things he gets right every day

Redirecting Unworkable Behaviours

It is common to hear clients report that they use 'positive affirmations'. These are very popular and, in some ways, very useful. A positive affirmation is a statement made about yourself which is (not surprisingly) positive, spoken in the first person, and spoken in the present tense. For example, I might say, 'I am a strong and caring person and I live a wonderfully fulfilling life'.

In general I am in favour of these affirmations as they are better than the 'negative affirmations' which many Auto Pilots generate.

Our Auto Pilot has a profound ability to fill our minds with beliefs, assumptions, opinions and attitudes. Most of these are helpful and contribute to our wellbeing. In other words, they work. Unfortunately, our Auto Pilot is incapable of telling the difference between things that work and things that don't work. We also have a tendency to pay attention to things that are unpleasant, as discussed in *Chapter 2*. This tendency means that our Auto Pilot often learns to be our harshest critic. It tells us stories that are uncomplimentary, critical and contrary to our wellbeing.

These stories are seductive because they include an element of truth, so it does not occur to our Auto Pilot that there might be another side to the story. It is incredibly common for people to have negative self-beliefs as a result of their Auto Pilot accidentally editing their life experiences so that they hold beliefs about their own behaviour that are unworkable. An over-critical or demanding parent can also train their child's Auto Pilot to believe that they are stupid, worthless and will never amount to anything. These negative affirmations undermine our confidence and tend to become self-fulfilling prophesies.[9]

Positive affirmations are an attempt to undermine the harm done by these negative affirmations.

9. Martin Seligman's authoritative work *Learned Helplessness* gives a powerful insight into this phenomenon. However, his follow-up work *Learned Optimism* has been a contributing factor to my beliefs and opinions.

However, the approach taken in this book is very different. This book advocates *thinking* in general, rather than mere positive thinking. As discussed in *Chapter 2*, if we consider our life as a 'pile of stuff' and engage our Clever Brain in reflecting on the entire pile, then we will be empowered to appreciate those things that work (the positives), influence those things that don't work that we can change (shift negatives to positives), and accept those things that don't work over which we have no control (accepting the negatives).

You may remember from *Chapter 2* the metaphor of the nail in the foot. That example showed that our Auto Pilot has a built-in tendency to pay attention to things that don't work, are painful, or are unpleasant. Some of these things, like the nail, are really important. If you only focus on the positives, there is a risk that those things that do not work (the negatives) are less likely to be in your minds and therefore less able to be influenced by your Clever Brain. In other words, they are likely to be repeated by your Auto Pilot. While it is important to notice and draw attention to the positives (those things that work), it is also important to identify things that don't work so that they can be influenced by your Clever Brain where possible.

A CLEVER BRAIN EXERCISE...

Russ Harris provides an excellent exercise in his book *ACT Made Simple* for dealing with negative stories and beliefs.

1. Name one of your negative stories or beliefs and write that name on a clipboard.
2. Hold the clipboard firmly with both hands in front of your eyes so that it touches the tip of your nose. In this position

the story occupies all of your available resources, restricts your ability to see anything else, and its proximity to your eyes means that even the story itself is blurred and out of focus! This represents how powerfully your Auto Pilot uses the grains of truth in this story to distract you, upset you, and reduce your ability to be the best person that you can be. Please note that your Auto Pilot does not do this with any malign intent.

3. Place the clipboard on your lap and acknowledge that it is available if you do need it in the future.

4. Fill in the rest of the story – defuse the true negative aspects of the story by realistically and truthfully considering the entire story.

The power of this exercise is that it allows your Clever Brain to awaken. Your Clever Brain has the capacity to use logic, determine right from wrong, solve problems, access your values, and consider the consequences to change the programmed story.

SETTING A GOOD EXAMPLE

As with any enthusiastic but stupid employee, it is important to avoid accidentally teaching your Auto Pilot the wrong attitudes and behaviours. While positive reinforcement and redirecting unworkable behaviours will help encourage more workable behaviours, if you set a bad example as the manager, you are unwittingly training your Auto Pilot to act contrary to your values and create more 'Oh no!' moments.

What does this look like in practice? The two biggest signs that your Clever Brain is setting a bad example for your Auto Pilot are double standards and values-contrary behaviour.[10]

---

10. Keep in mind that both of these scenarios can occur when you are on Auto Pilot, and are examples of unworkable behaviour you need to redirect. The point I want to make is that if you *consciously* set double standards and don't act in line with your values, you are further training your Auto Pilot to automatically repeat these same behaviours.

How many times have you observed someone, your boss, spouse, or parent, tell you to do one thing and then go off and do exactly the opposite? The 'do as I say, not as I do' mentality is incredibly common, and incredibly irritating. To ensure you're setting the right example for your Auto Pilot, you must be alert for your own double standards. Another idea is telling those around you that you are seeking feedback and will acknowledge it when it is offered.

The other area is values-contrary behaviour, something almost every child in the world has seen in their parents. I recall when we were selling our house some years ago and the agent asked what we expected to achieve as a selling price. We gave him a number which was somewhat higher than that which we had discussed over the breakfast table in the company of our, then, nine-year-old son. His (thankfully private) horrified aside to me was, 'Mummy just lied to that man!' We had unwittingly demonstrated behaviour contrary to our value of telling the truth – a value which we had relentlessly demonstrated and avowed to him his entire life. His innocent confusion led to another breakfast-table conversation which, in relatively simple terms, introduced the concept of values dilemmas. He quickly realised that speaking the truth is a value which rates very highly, and that our compromise of that value was not undertaken lightly.

Your Auto Pilot is like your child watching at the breakfast table – very open and observant and very willing to learn, so ensure you're teaching the right lessons.

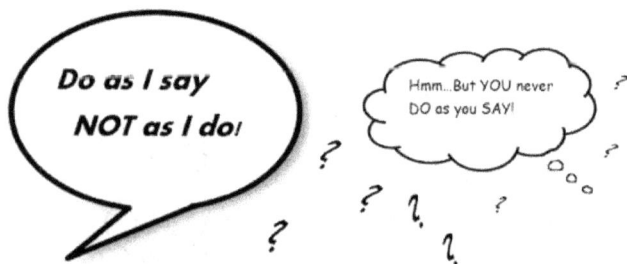

A CLEVER BRAIN EXERCISE...

Try to identify your recurring double standards and other inconsistencies between your values and your actions. Just becoming more aware of these issues will help you in the journey of retraining your Auto Pilot.

How to manage your Auto Pilot

Now these areas of management are all very good in theory, but how do you actually train your Auto Pilot? I've found one of the easiest, and most effective, ways is simply by talking to him.

Talking to your Auto Pilot

As my experience with this model developed, both as a therapist and as a person, I realised that I had intuitively begun having one-way conversations with my Auto Pilot. I was, in fact, 'telling' my Auto Pilot what I wanted him to do. These one-way conversations have now become a natural part of my life and I 'talk' to my Auto Pilot many times every day. When I describe this experience to clients, it is not uncommon for them to get that look on their face, the 'Riiiight… isn't that crazy talk?!'. I try to reassure them that, as long as your Auto Pilot doesn't talk back, then it is not crazy. And if it *is* crazy, it's crazy in a way that seems to work. A saying I came across many years ago is, 'There's a pleasure sure in being mad which none but madmen know'. As I experience my rich, full and meaningful life, I am happy to admit that, if I am mad, I would prefer that over any form of miserable sanity.

My daily, and now habitual, behaviour is to pay deliberate attention to what my Auto Pilot is doing. How? This comes down to the mindfulness we discussed in the previous chapter, and it gets easier the more you practice it, even if it is invisible to others. As you realise that your Auto Pilot carries out thousands of actions every day, your Clever Brain will have plenty of opportunities to praise or redirect him, with far more potential for praise than redirection.

Some clients initially report that actually talking to their Auto Pilot is not an intuitive thing to do. However, they almost always report that it gets easier as they deliberately practice it. This practice effect is yet another example of the power of the Auto Pilot. It is capable of learning to tell your Clever Brain to wake up and pay attention. In other words, if you use your Clever Brain to deliberately awaken itself, your Auto Pilot will eventually learn to do it for you. In my experience this has resulted in me talking to my Auto Pilot a lot. When I reflect on how often I talk to my Auto Pilot, it feels like I talk to him at least a hundred times a day. Happily, most of those silent observations are of a positive nature because my Clever Brain realises that my Auto Pilot is incredibly good at most of what he does, and incredibly motivated to do the right thing. My job is to supervise and encourage to give him the opportunity to be the best he can be.

A CLEVER BRAIN EXERCISE...

If you haven't already, take time now to find an identity for your Auto Pilot. Have a chat – and perhaps give this constant and loyal 'buddy' of yours a name.

The power of Dream Sheets

Beyond simply talking to your Auto Pilot, there are other exercises you can do that both awaken your Clever Brain and give your Auto Pilot clear instructions about the behaviours you want to create and the habits you want to develop.

My wife and I stumbled upon one of these by accident. We are, in general, fans of technology, and when we went overseas in 1994 we bought one of the very first generation of palm top computers in the Duty Free shop at the airport – a Hewlett Packard Psion. It had a monochrome stylus driven touch screen in the top of the oyster case, and a tiny keyboard in the bottom half.

After charging it up we sat by the pool at our resort familiarising ourselves with this new gadget and we set out the next ten years of our lives in a spreadsheet. We imagined the milestones and achievements we might experience from year to year. Then we saved it and, holiday over, forgot about it.

Twelve years and many generations of technology later we were spring cleaning and came across this long discarded and out-dated little machine. Packed away in a bag it still had its power cord so we fired it up to briefly reflect on how much technology had changed. Without any real searching we came across that old spreadsheet and were incredulous at how it had predicted our future. We had both completed our qualifications, we had had a child, we had made a million dollars through buying real estate, and we had relocated to Queensland and lived in a luxury home without a mortgage. The ten years covered by our 'Dream Spreadsheet' had also been relatively free of adversity.

At that time it did not occur to us that the ten-year plan had expired and that we were at the beginning of a rapid and significant decline in our fortunes. With the wisdom of hindsight we now suspect that the absence of clear goals or any form of Dream Sheet may well have contributed to the almost complete reversal of our financial wellbeing.

While there is no science to support the idea of a Dream Sheet, the act of creating one does activate the parts of our mind that are the domain of our Clever Brain. Dream Sheets force us to use our imagination, consider our values and solve problems, all part of the role of the Clever Brain or manager.

Meanwhile this also takes advantage of the tendency of your Auto Pilot to follow instructions and learn habits. To date, your Auto Pilot has been randomly programmed by environmental influences. By creating new influences, like a Dream Sheet, which lead you towards your values, you are reprogramming your Auto Pilot to learn the behaviours required to create a life based on those values.

In other words, rather than permitting your present and your future to be determined by your habits or random chance, this is one way to deliberately influence your circumstances and change your life in accordance with your values by tapping into the power of your Clever Brain.

A CLEVER BRAIN EXERCISE…

Consider starting a Dream Sheet, a dream book, or a series of dream books. It is interesting that the mere process of paying attention to 'dreams' will help identify your values and life goals. Dream books are usually pictorial but they don't have to be – I have seen many good Pinterest boards filled with motivational, inspirational and values-based quotes.

Go the old-fashioned way and use a scrap book, or use the many platforms now at your disposal with technology.

As for us, we are on the road to creating our next million dollars (still quite a long journey!), we are deliberately influencing our physical health, and we mindfully use our Clever Brains to deliver a rich, full and meaningful life together.

We now review and update our 'Dream Sheet' on an annual basis.

Journaling

There is a time-honoured tradition for some people of keeping a diary. Now, I've never been one to keep a diary, but I am beginning to appreciate the potential value that such an activity could bring to our psychological behaviours.

Journaling, scrapbooking, and diarising are ways of getting your experiences and behaviour down on paper for later reflection. If you journal – for your own eyes, of course – you have the opportunity to reflect on the manner in which your environment, your experiences, and other people, have influenced your thoughts, your emotions and your reactions.

It is also a way of reflecting on your own behaviour that is different from just meditating, thinking over things, or talking about it with other people, because the act of writing your experiences and recollections down activates both of your brains in a couple of interesting ways. Your Auto Pilot will be effectively distracted by the complicated act of writing, and that will allow your Clever Brain to start to process and contribute, to some degree, to what you're writing down.

The act of writing has a permanence attached to it. If you reflect on your day just by keeping it in your mind, then you are prey to your Auto Pilot editing your reflections. He will certainly edit which of those reflections remains as a memory and how accurately even those memories might be retained.

When you journal something relatively soon after the event, then you have the potential to capture some of your automatic experiences, responses, actions, thoughts and emotions for later, sober, contemplation.

So journaling, in and of itself, is not a bad thing to do. But journaling without reflection on those journal entries is not as powerful. It is the reflection that gives power to journaling. Reflection can cover what worked, what didn't work, what was in line with your values, what made you feel good, and what made you feel uncomfortable.

DEVELOPING A MANAGERIAL STYLE TO MANAGE YOUR AUTO PILOT

Anyone who has to manage people in an organisation knows that employees can be at different stages of development and will require different styles in order to be effectively managed. Similarly, our Auto Pilots have different stages of functionality and an awareness of these stages can be helpful in managing you own Auto Pilot.

The Functionality Matrix, a proposed model for understanding and managing your Auto Pilot, is as follows:

FUNCTIONALITY MATRIX

This grid sets out the alternative Auto Pilot and Clever Brain states depending on the degree of awareness of the behaviour (the vertical axis) and the effectiveness of that behaviour (the horizontal axis).

Q1 Normally Functional

Happily, the majority of people live in the "You" quadrant. In this quadrant our behaviour is comfortingly and invisibly workable. This Normally Functional quadrant is the world where our Auto Pilot "gets it right" and our Clever Brain is normally fast asleep. In this quadrant our learned behaviours deliver desirable outcomes which are in line with our values. This is the place where managing your Auto Pilot consists of noticing what works. The "You" quadrant is the place where we fall under the Illusion of Control. Here is where our Auto Pilot shines and often appears to be intelligent. People living in this quadrant rarely experience duress or upset. Their experience is one of relative peace and satisfaction. In terms of managing your Auto Pilot, the Normally Functional quadrant is one of the significant places where a rich, full, and meaningful life can be found. Paying attention to the Normally Functional quadrant makes our otherwise invisible but functional behaviour available for us to appreciate and perpetuate.

Q2 Abnormally Functional

This book is an attempt to make the next quadrant available to you. The Abnormally Functional quadrant is the arena where the Clever Brain is awake and intentionally sets out to influence your Auto Pilot. This quadrant is the domain of non-automatic behaviour. Unfortunately such behaviour is unlikely to be fluid and relaxed. Similar to Sheldon in the Big Bang Theory, such deliberate Clever Brain behaviour is often awkward and hesitant. Occupying this quadrant is very hard work. Typically your Auto Pilot will actively try to persuade you to leave this quadrant as it is a world of novelty and deliberate change. It is, however, the place where meaningful and intentional change exists. From the perspective of managing your Auto Pilot this quadrant is where we can initiate deliberate change.

Q3 Abnormally Dysfunctional

The Abnormally Dysfunctional quadrant is a relatively, and thankfully, rare experience for most people. This is the domain where the Clever Brain is in charge but it directs us away from our values in a deliberate and pathological manner. Called the Hitler quadrant, it is the home of psychopaths who are willing to do anything to achieve their own ends. If you suspect that you live in this quadrant then this book will be of minimal value to you other than as a way to better understand how to understand other people and potentially manipulate them more effectively. Thankfully such people are so self-obsessed that they are unlikely to perceive any way that they might benefit from a book like this – so don't tell them about it!

Q4 Normally Dysfunctional

The Homer Simpson quadrant is another domain frequently visited by normal human beings. In the Normally Dysfunctional quadrant our Auto Pilot is, again, in charge, but the outcomes are not in line with our values and therefore frequently do not work. Named after Fox Studios' hapless but well-intentioned Homer Simpson, it is the domain of behaviour which is innocently out of line with our values and which is usually only recognised when our Clever Brain awakens and realises, just too late, that we have messed up. In the terminology of this book that results in an "Oh No!" moment. In Homer's world that is known as a "Do'h!" moment. From the perspective of managing our Auto Pilot this is the domain where mindful awareness rules but is very rare. Here is the place where we can interrupt our maladaptive automatic behaviours and give ourselves opportunities to move closer to our values.

An awareness of your own levels of awareness and functionality is one of the core principles of this book. Whilst complex, this matrix is an attempt to clarify and reframe the states of mind we might occupy and to empower you to maximise each element.

CHAPTER SUMMARY

- Beyond using your Clever Brain to choose values-based behaviours in the moment, you need to actively train your Auto Pilot so it can take over these workable behaviours and make them automatic.

- To do this, you need to manage your Auto Pilot through positive reinforcement, redirecting unworkable behaviours and setting a good example.

- By observing your Auto Pilot, you have the opportunity to notice when your Auto Pilot gets it right. Taking delight in the behaviours which work is legitimate and important positive feedback and, from a behavioural perspective, it is likely to increase the frequency of those behaviours.

- Beyond simply focusing on the positive, you need to redirect unworkable behaviours.

- It is also important to avoid accidentally teaching your Auto Pilot the wrong attitudes and behaviours through avoiding double standards and values-contrary behaviour.

- You can manage your Auto Pilot in a variety of ways. Some include talking to your Auto Pilot, writing to him in a journal or letters, and creating Dream Sheets.

- Your growing awareness of your own behaviour and its workability is summarised in the Functionality Matrix. This can be a helpful tool to remind you of where you are in terms of managing your Auto Pilot and activating you Clever Brain.

GREAT

((CHANGE))

MAKER

WHY CLEVER PEOPLE
DO DUMB THINGS

CHAPTER 7:

ACTIVATE YOUR CLEVER BRAIN

TO CHANGE YOUR LIFE

I would hope that, having read this far, you are developing a sense of the power and efficacy of your Clever Brain.

If this is the case then you will also be developing a strong insight into the almost universal absence of Clever Brain activity in the world around you. While you will have noticed some people living according to their values, you will have seen countless examples of people unwittingly allowing their Auto Pilot to move them away from their values.

Building Clever Brain relationships

As the philosopher John Donne said, 'No man is an island'. So while we can awaken our own Clever Brains and reprogram our own Auto Pilots, the value of this is multiplied when we incorporate this knowledge into the way we interact with others.

One common example of where our Auto Pilot takes over is in an argument. Our Auto Pilot controls our habitual behaviours, emotions, personality, and the maintenance of our bodily functions. And, while our Auto Pilot is a superb 'doing' machine, it lacks any ability to think. If you consider an argument, you will almost always discover that an argument demonstrates habitual behaviours, is emotionally based, that we have a particular style in which we argue, and that we experience bodily responses similar to the fight or flight response which can only come from our Auto Pilot.

So an argument is, essentially, two Auto Pilots attacking each other until one prevails or both run out of steam, an experience that leaves both parties dissatisfied without any real understanding of how that dissatisfaction came about. If the louder voice or stronger personality prevails, then both Auto Pilots learn a set of rules relating to arguments which can result in, at worst, a co-dependent relationship or a failed one. If the arguments result in stalemates or randomly determined 'wins' to both sides, then that relationship is likely to be a tumultuous one. If one party 'learns' not to argue then passive aggression sets in and both parties develop a sense of frustration and intolerance for the other.

By contrast, the role of our Clever Brain is to provide logical thought, a moral sense of right and wrong, an ability to solve problems, access to our values, and a capacity to consider the consequences of our actions. When you think of what most people call an argument, I suspect that you will find an almost complete absence of these activities.[11]

Consequently, we can assume that relating to others from our Clever Brain, rather than our Auto Pilot, will result in fewer heated arguments and swifter conflict resolution. Earlier in this book I introduced to you the Illusion of Control. You may recall that the idea that you are 'in control' is invisibly and universally generated by the fact that your Auto Pilot does a really good job of being 'you' – even when 'being you' doesn't work. In the many conversations with clients in my practice I have found that the Illusion of Control is so powerful that it leads us to believe that we are acting logically, even when we are not.

We believe that we are acting in a morally correct manner, even when we are not, we believe that we are creatively solving problems when we are in fact merely applying the habitual rules and principles that we have learnt throughout our lives. We assume that our actions and behaviours are in line with our most important values, and we frequently act in a manner which has unpleasant outcomes in the future. All of these anomalies typically only become evident *after the fact*, when we have an 'Oh No!' moment indicating that our Clever Brain has just woken up and, at last, we have all of those higher mental functions available to us. Clearly, activating your Clever Brain deliberately and frequently will reduce the number of times you act illogically, immorally, in a problem generating manner, contrary to your values, and in a manner that will result in adverse outcomes further down the track.

---

11. It is important to recognise that there is a type of argument which does not meet the above criteria. Scholarly or philosophical arguments and debates, when examined, can be seen to contain all the elements of the Clever Brain. They follow rules, have form and function, and are an attempt to reach the most appropriate conclusion. As a young man I took part in many organised social debates. I recall them being great fun and that all parties realised that it was the process that mattered rather than the outcome. Once the debate was adjudicated (always by a disinterested and qualified third party) everyone would shake hands and have a laugh together over some of the arguments raised.

This comes back to the Influence Diagram and the idea of using mindfulness to either catch yourself at the Invisible Decision Point, or catch yourself carrying out unworkable behaviours and changing that behaviour as you go.

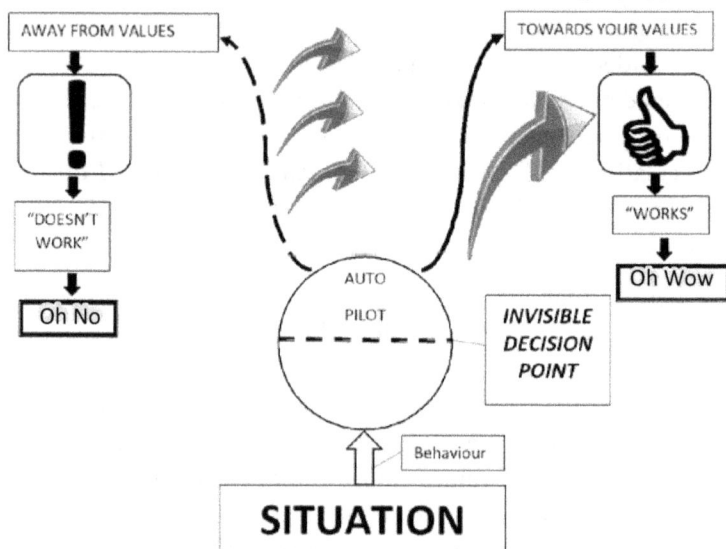

As you now know, assuming responsibility for your Auto Pilot's actions as they unfold is the key to preventing an 'Oh no!' moment, and involving your Clever Brain so you can direct your actions is the key to having more 'Oh wow!' moments.

This is how my much-loved partner and I have built a relationship where we don't argue. Instead, we disagree in a manner which brings about values-based results almost every time we disagree. I am the first to admit that our relationship is not perfect, but I am also a staunch supporter of the use of a Clever Brain to make a relationship as perfect as it can be.

A CLEVER BRAIN EXERCISE...

I recently came across a truism about creating a happy relationship, 'When you are wrong, admit it. When you are right, shut up!' While I do not wholly agree with this 'rule', it is far more practical than the alternative which might be, 'When you are wrong, argue. When you are right, rub it in!'

Try experimenting with, 'When you are wrong, admit it. When you are right, shut up.' See what happens and reflect on how you feel and how the people around you react.

Of course, I am not telling you to keep quiet in all situations as this would not be true to yourself and can quickly turn into passive aggression. However, it is useful to experiment with new behaviour so that you can get a handle on how to address different circumstances. When you do find yourself engaged in an argument or heated discussion, try taking a step back and deliberately try to activate your Clever Brain – think of your values and the consequences of your behaviours and try to find an effective resolution to the issue at hand.

Rules of engagement

One of my favourite fictional characters is Sheldon from The Big Bang Theory. While I do not hold him up as a paragon of virtue, his approach to the 'roommate agreement' (incredibly irritating to those in his social environment) can be seen to invariably resolve arguments. The frustrations shown by the other parties are clearly a demonstration of their emotional Auto Pilots not having taken into account the rules of engagement to which they earlier agreed. The humour inherent in The Big Bang Theory relates to the extreme nature of Sheldon's personality and I am not recommending that such pedantry be aspired to by my clients or my readers. However, there is value in having these formal agreements in place before disagreements arise.

Rules of engagement have two functions. First, they have the potential to supersede the automatic programming of any one person's Auto Pilot in the household. Second, if adhered to by the entire family, they have the capacity to reprogram the Auto Pilot of any person in the household in mutually agreed ways.

The rules of engagement that my wife and I originally agreed to when we had the ugly argument referred to earlier in this book include an agreement that either party could call a thirty-second timeout if they felt negative emotion emerging on either side of the discussion. At the end of the timeout both parties had to agree on the topic under discussion before either were permitted to continue the discussion. Our experience has been that our Auto Pilots eventually learnt this rule of engagement to the point that it is almost never needed in our relationship today.

Another example is having rules of engagement around how you deliver critical comments. Not so long ago my now thirteen-year-old son went to a brilliant Super Camp, organised by the amazing Heather Yelland (greensupercamp.com.au), and had an incredible learning experience. One of the things he came home with was a way of delivering criticism called OTFD, which stands for Observe,

Think, Feel and Desire. An OTFD statement might be, 'This is what I have *observed*, this is what I *think* it means, this is what I *feel* as a result of that, and this is what I would *desire* to be different.'

Now, at almost no time in an OTFD statement does the word 'you' come into it; it's almost all 'I' phrases. And that means the individual uttering the OTFD statement is taking complete responsibility for their own behaviours and not trying to inflict their opinions on the other person. In my opinion an OTFD statement activates a person's Clever Brain. And there can be real and meaningful interpersonal change developed as a result of this.

The rules of engagement that you develop might be different. The important thing is that they are developed by your Clever Brain in an unemotional environment – through individual consultation, suggestion boxes or round table family conversations.

Now, these kinds of rules of engagement are relatively simple to create within a two-person relationship. They are a little more difficult to maintain, but they are a very powerful way of reducing the harm of harsh words. They become increasingly difficult in multiple-person relationships such as work and blended families, but the underlying assumptions still apply – and it often only takes one Clever Brain to interrupt an ugly argument.

FAMILY MEETINGS

Within families, I am a huge fan of family meetings: reasonably regular and reasonably structured meetings where every member of the family gets to have a time-limited say, usually managed by some form of token.

My favourite token is the clockwork egg timer, where each person can advance it to three minutes and have their three minutes of speech, but they are only allowed to speak while they have the egg timer. Once their three minutes are up, they have to stop and hand it to the next person. This a deliberately controlled democratic activity, therefore the content raised by each member of the family can be unpredictable. This is a *good* thing. If teen pregnancy or easy access to illicit substances are not on your agenda, but your fourteen year old raises such an issue, you have just opened a channel of communication that might otherwise have festered or resulted in unexpected and unfortunate outcomes. Family meetings are not for the faint hearted – but then neither is this book.

If there are enough members in the family – and you need three or more for this to work – then each person takes turns rotating as the chairperson. The chairperson is not allowed to have an opinion; all they do is manage the rules. And the brilliant outcomes are that it gives everybody a say, it obliges everybody to think about what they are going to say because they only have three minutes to say it, and it requires everybody else to shut up while the speaker is having their three minutes. It can be a real deal changer.

A number of years back, my wife and I took some international students into our home for a year. We had a very interesting experience early in the time these wonderful young women stayed with us. Someone in the household was overusing our internet bandwidth download allowance. That meant that we all went back to dial-up speed for a substantial proportion of the month that followed.

Now, I suspect that many Auto Pilot parents would have made some judgments, put some rules into place, and potentially made everybody miserable, because only one person was causing the problem. It occurred to us to hold a family meeting, put this issue on the table and seek input from the other members of our family, as temporary as it was, including those two extra young women.

To our disbelief, one of the young women immediately said, 'I know how to fix it. I was downloading. And instead of downloading movies, I will now hire them from the video shop.' The problem was solved, without any required inputs or aggression from either of the adults in the room.

Awakening other Clever Brains

What you may have begun to realise through reading this book is that, beyond awakening your own Clever Brain with these techniques, you also have the power to influence other people's Auto Pilots.

How? It is my opinion that an argument is almost impossible to sustain even if just one Clever Brain is working. The typical course of an argument is for it to run its ugly course and for both Clever Brains to eventually wake up after the event and generate self-recriminations and regret. However, by engaging your Clever Brain, you can simply end the argument (as in the example with my colleague and his stapler in an earlier chapter), or you can awaken the *other* person's Clever Brain as well.

So how can you activate someone else's Clever Brain? I've found writing to be a very effective way to awaken our Clever Brain when emotions are running high.

Writing letters

We humans are the only species with the ability to communicate in abstract terms. Our language is incredibly complex and we take it for granted – even when it fails us. It has been my observation that most people believe that the best way to communicate is to 'talk things over'. It is also my observation that very few such conversations actually deliver a satisfactory result. My opinion is that verbal communication tends to fail because it is so darned hard.

Consider the normal English-speaking person's vocabulary. Of the more than 300,000 words in the English language (estimates range up to 1 million depending on the definition of 'words') the average person has an available vocabulary of up to 35,000 words. That means that every time we speak we need to select the right words, put them in the right order and tense, speak them at the right volume and speed, use the appropriate light and shade, breathe, and use gestures, body language, and facial expressions appropriate to our meaning. Then reverse the process for the person receiving the message. It is an incredible testament to our Auto Pilot that we can speak at all! This unbelievably complicated process now needs to be considered against a background of emotions and conflicting beliefs.

Clearly talking to other people is an activity which we should take very seriously. Unfortunately it is way too complex and rapid for our Clever Brain to properly manage – particularly when emotions run high. In my psychology practice it is common to have people express their difficulties communicating with the people they love. I often recommend that clients consider experimenting with the written word rather than entrusting their Auto Pilot with the important task of getting in touch with their partner's Clever Brain. Occasionally they try it. It almost always makes a difference and that difference is almost always positive.

I recall one man who, as he told me his story, wept almost continuously. He described how his thirty-year marriage had quietly faded away until he felt that its end was inevitable. They rarely fought but they rarely spoke either. He was convinced that, now he had retired, his wife was planning to leave him. Having taken his history and determined that it was appropriate, I recommended that he write his wife a love letter. My recommendation was that it had to be hand written, it needed to satisfy his needs regarding what he wanted to say to her, and that he could not be with her when she read it. In other words, it required his Auto Pilot to be distracted by the complex act of hand writing, it had to reflect the input of his Clever Brain, and it would require her Clever Brain to interpret his written words while her Auto Pilot was distracted by the difficult act of decoding his writing.

I was unable to see this man again for about four weeks, but when he did return the change in him was astounding. For a moment I was unsure that I was remembering the right client. He was smiling and confident. He reported that the letter had been difficult to write and that he had been scared to give it to her. He had bared his heart and written about his hope for their future. He handed her the envelope and asked her to read it, then he left to play golf. His anxiety ruined his golf game and he returned four hours later to find her waiting for him at the front door. He explained to me that he was sure that she was going to end their marriage at that point. As he walked towards her he realised that she was crying and his apprehension deepened. When he was close to her she embraced him and said, 'I never knew you felt that way'. In the hours and days that followed, they found that they were able to communicate at a level that had never existed in all the years that they had been together. While he had been working and she had raised children, their Auto Pilots had been able to muddle through. Once he retired and the children left home, their Auto Pilots had no idea what to do or say. It was the activation of his Clever Brain that led to her Clever Brain being engaged, which allowed them to connect with their values.

A CLEVER BRAIN EXERCISE...

If you need to approach a difficult situation with someone, write them a letter. Of course, you shouldn't write this letter when you are in a highly agitated and emotional state. Take the time to clearly state where you are coming from and how you are having difficulty with your values. Perhaps get someone to read your letter before sending it – however, if the process of writing the letter alone has clarified some of the issues for you, you may just decide to rip it up. It's up to you.

Mind/Body Connection

Throughout this book I have referred to managing interpersonal relationships by invoking your Clever Brain. I am now going to open the subject up to the relationship of your body with your brain.

As a student learning psychology twenty-six years ago I was exposed to the time-honoured philosophical question about the mind/body connection. Are the mind and body separate? Or are they a mutual part of a single entity? Is there a relationship between the two?

While there are arguments for and against this philosophical debate, after more than twenty years in professional practice I have now formed the opinion that the mind and body are inextricably linked and have a phenomenal impact on one another.

One argument in favour of this connection is the anxiety response, or the fight or flight response. For example, when most people see a great big black spider scuttling across their hand, one of the immediate reactions is that their heart rate increases. I don't believe for a moment that spiders have some form of clever neurotoxin on the bottom of their feet that can stimulate your autonomic nervous system to create a change in your heart rate. What these people are actually experiencing is a psychological reaction to their environment that manifests itself in a change in their physiology. In other words, their mind has increased their heart rate in order to prepare them to run away from or fight the threat. Consider also the act of falling in love. I doubt that anyone who has experienced this phenomenon would doubt that this emotional and psychological response has physiological connotations – none of them deliberate, and most of them pleasant. Sadly many of us have experienced unrequited love, and that brings with it an entirely different set of physiological and behavioural consequences.

Now if we continue on the assumption that the mind has some impact on the body, and your Auto Pilot is the brain that's usually in control, this means that a significant part of your health and happiness is being determined by your Auto Pilot. Fortunately, you can train your Auto Pilot to interact with your body differently.

When I began exploring the two brains framework a few years ago, I remember waking one morning with a severe headache. Now, as one of the luckiest people in the world, it is very rare for me to get a headache, but every now and then I get a real doozy. These headaches are definitely not migraines but they are disabling. Like most people I have a very busy life – headaches just don't fit in and they obviously don't work for me. Now for various philosophical, physiological and psychological reasons I would rather not take medications if I can help it.

On this particular day, as I lay in bed wondering how I would get through my gruelling day with a debilitating headache, a number of things came together in my Clever Brain. The connections that I made revealed my absolute belief of the interaction between my mind and my body.

I wondered why I would have a headache. I haven't been drunk for twenty-five years so I obviously wasn't hung-over; I pay attention to the amount of water I drink so it was unlikely that I was dehydrated; and I was pretty certain that I didn't have any type of brain disorder. So I was left with only one option… my Auto Pilot had done something. As Sherlock Holmes says, 'When you have eliminated the impossible, whatever remains, however improbable, must be the truth'.

So I had an internal discussion with myself. I said to my Auto Pilot, 'I have a blinding headache and it's not working for me. I think it is because you have accidentally screwed something up. I would really appreciate it if you could take as much time as you need to go about reversing what you have done. I have no idea what you have to do; it might be my blood pressure, my brain chemistry, neurological – whatever it is, please fix it and I will let you know when the headache is gone.'

Despite my headache, I got up and started to go about my daily business. About three minutes later I realised that my headache was gone and I immediately thanked my Auto Pilot and asked him to stop making adjustments relating to my headache.

It has been over six years since that particular headache and I have continued to have one or two headaches each year. Each time I have engaged and trained my Auto Pilot to help me out. I am delighted to tell you that this training has meant that all I usually need to do now when I get a headache is tell him, 'Can you make this headache go away please, Buddy?' – and within twenty seconds it is gone.

The medical fraternity refer to this as the 'placebo effect' and, while they don't give it much credence, there is some emerging respect for this phenomenon. It frequently frustrates the pharmacological industry when they take a new drug to clinical trials and the experimental group who are, unwittingly, taking the sugar pill, experience better outcomes than the group who are taking the pill containing the new drug.

I retain my belief that it is a profoundly important part of managing the relationship with one of your key life partners – your body. If you are overweight, unfit, have some form of illness or another ailment, there is some capacity to have a psychological impact on it if you choose. If you try to direct your Auto Pilot to do what he can to fix it, then there are two potential outcomes. First, your Auto Pilot will do his best to change it but will be unable to help, or second, he might just be able to fix it.[12]

---

12. Please note that I very strongly recommend that if you are ill you should go to a medical doctor. I am not attempting to trivialise medical conditions in any way, shape or form.

A CLEVER BRAIN EXERCISE...

Take your own pulse. It's easiest to place your left index, middle, and ring fingers on your right wrist directly below the ball of your thumb. You'll need a watch or clock or phone with a seconds indicator. Count the beats for 15 seconds and then multiply the result by 4. The resulting number is your heart rate, the number of times your heart beats each minute. Regardless of the number (if you are relaxed and restful and it is above 80 then you might consider talking to your GP about it) please do a short mindfulness/relaxation exercise. Perhaps imagine being in a safe, secure, comfortable place and deeply immerse yourself in that imaginary experience. It can be very effective to pay attention to your environment in a detailed and trivial way with your eyes closed. Listening to sounds you would otherwise not have noticed, and experiencing sensations that you normally don't notice such as your feet in your shoes, or your jewellery touching your skin. After a few short moments of such deliberately relaxing concentration, take your pulse again. It is very common for the number to have reduced by a surprising number of beats. This is a clear demonstration of your mind influencing your body. Without realising it you have influenced your Auto Pilot to change you own physiology.

There are some comforting restrictions on the placebo effect. You will not be in any danger of reducing your heart rate to zero. The basic programming in your Auto Pilot will ensure that you do not pass out due to lowering your heart rate to a dangerous level.

Managing your career

One other area where your Clever Brain could have significant impact is your career. I have met many people who are at the end of their working lives. And when they have reflected on why they spent thirty years in the same job, or drifted from job to job thirty times over the same thirty years, I have yet to hear any of them say, 'That was my plan; I actually set out some form of career manifestos that detailed where I would like to go during my working life.'

My own experience has been that in my mid-thirties, I reached a career crisis and I had no idea what I wanted to do. I knew that I did not want to go into middle management; I experienced that in my early twenties and made a hash of it. I didn't like the idea being sandwiched between senior management and front-line personnel.

By sheer chance I happened to bump into a psychologist who gave career advice. This man offered, very generously, to do an evaluation of my capacities, potential, preferences and interests. I quite happily took him up on that. The end result was that he was able to give me a very full and unemotional evaluation of my capacities, interests and vocational potential. And for better or for worse, that led me into psychology. The fact that I had a very deliberate, Clever Brain generated direction to take was one of the many things that motivated me through the eight years of hard work, heartache and trials that involved becoming a registered psychologist.

I have never regretted that career change. I now do a job that I am good at, that I totally enjoy and that I am probably going to be doing (even if it's only in a part-time capacity) as long as I'm physically and intellectually capable.

So how can your Clever Brain have input into your career choice? Start with the exercises from the previous chapter, which are valuable both for awakening your Clever Brain and managing your Auto Pilot. You could journal about the career you would like, write down on your Dream Sheet where you would like your career to go, or instruct your Auto Pilot to keep an eye out for any new opportunities.

Getting professional help, such as a career evaluation, intellectual assessment, or skills evaluation can also provide valuable Clever Brain feedback.

A CLEVER BRAIN EXERCISE...

Consider where your career now stands.

Do you have a plan?

Are you satisfied?

Do you like what you are doing and who you are doing it with?

If you answered 'Yes' to those questions then go no further, you are enjoying a rich, full, and meaningful career. If you answered 'no' to any or all, then actively use your Clever Brain to determine what is keeping you in that situation. It is scary how many people stay in a miserable set of circumstances because they have not actively considered their alternatives, and even if they do, how many allow their Auto Pilot to limit their evaluation of their alternatives.

THE ART OF BEING CONFUSED

Having been immersed in the approach detailed in this book for a number of years I became aware of an unexpected outcome within my own reactions. A little over a year ago, I realised that I was living in a state of fairly deliberate and constant mild confusion. Rather than being a destabilising or uncomfortable state, I realised that I was gaining much comfort from the fact that my opinions were softening, that my beliefs were less rigidly held, and that I was becoming increasingly open to the ideas of other people.

It was an incredibly liberating realisation and lifted a huge burden of 'having to be right' from my shoulders. Rather than trying to argue with other people, or trying to convince them that I was right and they were wrong, I discovered that by asking them to explain their point of view, one of two things happened. Either their explanation clarified my understanding or I realised that my thinking was incorrect, or they realised partway through their explanation that their argument was unsustainable and they tended to change their beliefs. Either way there was very little work required by me, I rarely made a fool of myself by arguing in favour of a wrong conclusion, and I tended to learn a lot more than I had before.

This strategy of being mildly confused is one which I recommend strongly for awakening your Clever Brain, especially when relating to others. There is an old adage which states that it is 'better to remain silent and be thought a fool than speak and remove all doubt'. I have found great pleasure in watching the changes that take place in a person's face, speech and body language when their Clever Brain is activated. I have drawn the conclusion that one of the things that most Auto Pilots have leant is to explain things to other people, and these 'programmed' explanations tend to be triggered by the other person being confused. It is sometimes difficult not to laugh when you observe another person's Clever Brain wake up part way through an Auto Pilot's explanation of a ridiculous opinion. Please note that it is never my intention to make someone else look stupid – they often do a fine job on their own!

A CLEVER BRAIN EXERCISE...

Experiment with uttering the phrase 'I'm confused' when you find yourself in difficult situations. This will encourage others to explain their situation and hopefully will bring some Clever Brain input into play – I think you will be surprised by what happens next.

A note of caution: There is an old saying which states 'In the land of the blind, the one-eyed man is King'. This saying infers that an advantage in perception will provide an equivalent environmental advantage. Some might believe that the ideas in this book have the potential to give you a perceived advantage over those around you by diffusing resentment, becoming more likeable and even influencing others. The danger lies in the possibility that you may be seen as manipulative or patronising. *Genuine* curiosity will defuse these dangers.

It is my belief that the cultivation of genuine curiosity is one of the keys to awakening your Clever Brain, and genuine curiosity isn't manipulative. It never ceases to amaze me how much I can learn from other people, even the stupid and opinionated. Using your Clever Brain to mindfully and creatively discover what is really going on is a liberating and empowering process.

And the more curious you get, the more open you will be to the information, ideas and approaches that can improve your quality of life. This is why you want to empower others to influence your Auto Pilot.

Chapter summary

- While we can awaken our own Clever Brains and reprogram our own Auto Pilots, the value of this is multiplied when we incorporate this knowledge into the way we interact with others.

- An argument is where two Auto Pilots are set against each other. Arguments, whether we like it or not, are often founded on habitual behaviours that are emotionally based. The trick is to intentionally wake up and engage our Clever Brain when things start to slip.

- Relating to others from our Clever Brain, rather than our Auto Pilot, will result in fewer heated arguments and swifter conflict resolution.

- Due to the connection between the mind and the body, your Auto Pilot can have unexpected influence on your health. The next time you have a health problem, ask your Auto Pilot to fix it and see what happens.

- By involving your Clever Brain in career decisions, you have the ability to choose a more fulfilling career path.

- You have the power to both overcome others' Auto Pilots and awaken their Clever Brains. Two good ways are to write letters and to practice the art of being confused.

GREAT
((CHANGE))
MAKER

CHAPTER 8:

TRAIN OTHERS TO INFLUENCE YOUR AUTO PILOT

In my early fifties I found myself living on acreage which backed onto a tiny nine-hole private golf course. I paid the membership fee and, having retired early, began to play a lot of golf. Very badly. I was consistently frustrated with my performance because my Auto Pilot had convinced me that I had a beautiful smooth swing. Why then did the ball never do what I wanted?

I finally bought a digital video camera and, with an expectation that my high opinion of my golf swing would be confirmed, I set myself up on the fairway behind my house and recorded myself hitting twenty or so balls. I then took the camera inside, connected it to the TV, and sat back to carefully observe the one or two things that might just be worthy of improvement.

I vividly recall the first few moments of that viewing experience. Alone in the house I actually found myself looking around to see if there was a Candid Camera team waiting to spring their trick on me. The only explanation for what I was watching was that someone had employed a comedian to dress like me and then deliver a series of Pythonesque parodies of a golf swing. I initially could not accept the fact that the guy haplessly chopping away at the ball, demonstrating no skill or finesse in any way, was me!

Finally I overcame my disbelief and began to accept that my game was terrible simply because my game was terrible. While I was a little demoralised and humiliated, I was also able to then take note of the defects in my swing, prioritise which elements I could realistically address first, and start addressing them. Gradually, over the next six months, I was finally able to start hitting the ball a reasonable distance and reasonably straight.

I have never again filmed myself playing golf because I achieved a level of skill which met my needs. I was able to play most courses in under 100 and achieve a handicap below the maximum limit of 27. My objective in any sporting endeavour is to be able to enjoy the activity at a level which is consistent with my age and the time I have available to play.

I share this anecdote to demonstrate that the way we perceive ourselves is almost never accurate. Our Auto Pilot is willing to delude us into thinking what it believes we want to know. However, we are surrounded by other people who have the ability to perceive our behaviours with far more clarity than we can, and it's essential to empower them to influence our Auto Pilots.

This is why, although I have always valued positive feedback, I have also valued and acted upon critical feedback even more. For example, at the end of my first semester at university at the age of thirty-seven, I was at the pub with some schoolmates commiserating over the past six months of study. One of my classmates, a quiet guy I will refer to as Clive, hit his relaxing third drink and commented to one and all that it was 'impossible to get a word in edgewise when Lindsay is in the room'.

Now I admit, I am an enthusiastic and demanding student who is *very* willing to ask questions and challenge things I cannot integrate with my existing knowledge. However, I am also *very* willing to take criticism on board and when we all made our way back to the same bar at the end of semester two, I asked Clive if he had found it easier to be heard during this semester. His emphatic and immediate response was a resounding 'No!' followed by another visit to what was, clearly, his bete noir.

When he finally wound down I reported to him that I had, in fact, changed my behaviour and that I now realised that the problem was not mine. During that second semester I had deliberately, and with great difficulty, withheld any classroom comments or questions until I had counted to ten, thus giving my classmates, and Clive, a head start. I had also reframed the manner in which I asked questions and made comments. Instead of saying 'I don't understand…' it had become my practice to say, 'Does anyone else understand…' and I was almost always met by a room full of bemused or encouraging expressions.

It became clear to me at that moment that my classmates would virtually all have happily gone through each class in relatively ignorant silence had it not been for my intervention. I made this observation to Clive and, as the next three years of study opened up, noted that an ever-increasing number of my class, many of whom remain friends today, began to enthusiastically challenge and question that which they had earlier taken for granted.

In yet another example, I started playing tennis when I was around forty years old. While I really loved it I was not a very good player. Enthusiastic and relatively fit, I held my own in social tennis but was wildly inaccurate. In my early fifties I joined a group of men playing every Saturday morning. I was clearly one of the weakest players but they generously tolerated me in the group.

After many years one of the very strong players finally became so frustrated with my playing that he began observing the way I played. He soon reported to me that he knew why I was so erratic. It appears that I was not 'watching the ball'. Now my Auto Pilot immediately knew what to do with this advice and went into defence and attack mode. 'Of course I watch the ball!' and I continued to spray balls all over the court. His frustration obviously continued to rise and he eventually took the time to explain what he meant. Apparently I was looking at the place on the court where I planned for the ball to land, rather than watching the ball's flight onto the face of the racquet. Over a decade later I now realise that my brilliant Auto Pilot is the only brain capable of calculating the incoming trajectory of a rapidly moving tennis ball, add to that complex information the action of the racquet in my hands, and simultaneously recall where the court and my opponent are in relation to me. With enough practice it will produce a potentially winning tennis shot. Unfortunately my Auto Pilot had learnt to ignore all the complex comparative trajectory stuff and was doggedly watching the only part of the equation which was stationary – the place where I wanted the ball to land!

Even with that wisdom carefully explained to me, my Auto Pilot persisted with his frustratingly inaccurate habitual behaviour. A relatively short time later I chanced to be watching a televised tennis tournament where the incredible Roger Federer was playing. The coverage included one of those amazing super slow-motion shots which, in this case, was a tight close up of Federer playing a forehand. To my amazement I watched this superb player's eyes track the flight of the ball all the way onto the face of his racquet and slightly past the point of contact, producing one of those unbelievably accurate and unreturnable shots for which he is justifiably famous. At last my Auto Pilot had evidence which it could not gainsay. I began to use my Clever Brain to deliberately try to override the entrenched habit of not watching the ball, and my accuracy began to dramatically improve.

It is now over ten years since my tennis partner gave me that wonderful advice. In general I have managed to influence my Auto Pilot to watch the ball onto the racquet. Unfortunately my Auto Pilot will never forget the habit of looking to where I want the ball to land, and it is very common for me to suddenly realise that my accuracy is gone, and I am hitting balls out or into the net way more often than I am willing to accept. I now realise what is happening and I literally stop myself on the court, having just delivered another unforced error, and I speak the words, 'Lindsay, watch the ball onto the racquet' with some force, and repeat them for the next five or six shots. The result is that my accuracy improves and I can again relax into the new habit, which delivers the outcomes that I desire. My game rises to the heady heights of mediocrity, and I take another small step along my path towards a rich, full and meaningful life.

In each of these examples, I was only able to become aware of my shortcomings through feedback from others. Overhearing a fellow student broke through my Auto Pilot's filter, seeing Federer watch the ball was irrefutable evidence, and seeing myself on video hitting a golf ball was undeniable proof that my self-perceptions were inaccurate. Either way, my Clever Brain needed external feedback to recognise what my Auto Pilot was getting wrong. And once it had that feedback, it was able to seek improvement and maintain vigilance to reduce the potential for my Auto Pilot to fall back into, or develop, habits which led me away from my values.

I encourage you to permit those you trust and respect to give your Clever Brain some feedback. This is way harder than it might sound. Your Auto Pilot has been doing the things that it has been doing for a long time. The power of habit can be overwhelming – ask any smoker. Meanwhile, your Clever Brain is a lazy brain and the effort required to influence your Auto Pilot can be huge – ask anyone who is overweight. Because of this it may take a few tries before the message sinks in – you might need to ask a couple of friends, a colleague, a coach, or even see a close-up of Roger Federer on TV. Whatever works for you, keep asking for feedback until it works. While your behaviours are almost invisible to you, they are clearly visible to those around you.

A CLEVER BRAIN EXERCISE…

Be daring and proactively ask for some feedback! It doesn't mean that you need to act on every piece of feedback or advice that you receive, but it does give you a fantastic opportunity to reflect and consider other people's viewpoints. If you feel that asking for feedback is a bit too brazen, then look for other clues that are offered as feedback such as the non-sought after spoken word, body language, and things people don't do. Don't forget the adage 'actions speak louder than words'.

FINDING A THERAPIST

If you decide that you would like to engage professional help, then I would like you to use your Clever Brain to do so. In most countries, you are legally and freely entitled to access therapy, in any way you wish. The challenge is, of all the people who offer therapy, how do you find one whose personality, style and therapeutic approach are going to suit you? Well, there's no easy way to answer that. The only real way to do it is to try. But there are some things to look out for in finding a therapist.

In the twenty years that I've been practicing as a psychologist, I've had many people refer to previous experiences with therapy, where they felt – and I'm aggregating a whole range of experiences – that the therapist was only interested in telling their own sad tale of woe; that the therapist was interested in listening, rather than giving any real form of constructive feedback; or that the therapist did not clarify or appear to use any sort of deliberate therapeutic model or approach.

Many of the people who reported those experiences were left a little confused and embittered by their experience. They reported that they had engaged in therapy with the expectation that they would receive specialist help from a trained and competent professional who would deliver meaningful outcomes. After all, if you went to the doctor with a broken arm, you would expect the arm to be professionally set, and you would expect, within a certain period of time, to have an intact arm. Therapy is much less cut-and-dried than setting a broken bone, but there are some very basic things that are worth considering.

The first is the role of the person referring you. If you are being referred to a therapist by a friend who has used that therapist, be very curious about the benefits they gained from the therapy. Some people get benefit just by being able to tell their story to a stranger – in other words, experiencing catharsis (or having a vent). If that is your friend's experience, then consider whether that's what you would expect from therapy. It can be worth giving catharsis a try, because almost everybody experiences some short-term benefit by being able to unload onto a non-judgmental stranger, in a confidential setting.

The second is that if you are being referred by a professional, such as your GP or a minister, then I would be interested in discovering why they were referring you to this particular person. If the response is, 'Well, I have referred many other people to them and they seem to like them', then that would sound an alarm to me. I would hope for some more substantial rationale for something as important as a mental health referral.

I would hope that the referrer would have some relatively empirical (provable) reason to refer. An example might be, 'This particular therapist provides some pretty solid feedback on their progress with their clients, and most people I send to them seem to improve'. Such a response might provide real comfort. There are many ways to measure progress in a solid and standardised way.

As mentioned earlier, one measure that I choose to use is the Outcome Rating Scale, or ORS. Designed by Scott Miller (www.scottdmiller.com) it is a session-by-session measure of a client's evaluation of their own wellbeing. And it has been my experience that this very simple, easy-to-use form clearly shows the progress of therapy in a numerical way. I have noticed that more and more of my colleagues are using progress measures such as the ORS to track each client's journey, and to evaluate their own performance.

If you find in your first session with a therapist that you don't like them or their approach, or you found that there was some serious impediment for you in engaging them, then please take that as a warning sign. I would encourage you, if you have the courage to do it, to acknowledge that to the therapist. Perhaps you could say, 'I am really sorry, but I feel as though there is a barrier here for me. I don't think this is going to work for me and I really think I need to talk to someone else.'

Now, there are only a couple of ways the therapist can respond to that. One could be in an open and sympathetic way. 'Well, I'm really sorry about that. I am sad that I couldn't help you. Is there anything you think I could do differently or better to improve my performance? Would you like me to find a colleague who might be able to help you?' That's the way I sincerely hope that any therapist would accept criticism.

If the therapist's response was anything other than that; if they became defensive, or angry, or teary, then I would hope that would be a salutary experience for you and you would realise that you were in the company of a therapist who needed a therapist.

If you found that your dissatisfaction with a therapist was soundly based and you had reservations about that therapist's training or professionalism, or a range of professional issues, then I would strongly recommend that you go back to the original referee and inform them.

THE ROLE OF ADVICE IN A THERAPEUTIC RELATIONSHIP

A common expectation of a therapist is that the therapist will tell you what to do. In other words, they will give you advice. Be very careful! A credible and seemingly powerful source providing advice, even when well-intentioned, can be dangerous. Many people have made bad buying decisions because the salesperson seemed to be 'such a nice person'.

Throughout your life, I'm sure you've been given advice on how you can improve yourself and your circumstances. In fact, on reflection you might realise that some of this advice relates to the activities your Auto Pilot has been performing on your behalf!

However, there are at least three unfortunate aspects of advice which many fail to grasp. Overall, these three factors mean that advice is almost always a waste of time.

The first factor is the perceptual funnel I referred to in *Chapter 4*. While this filter is very useful for reducing the amount of

environmental stimuli we receive, it is a significant barrier to good advice. If we filter it out then it can never impact on us!

The second frustrating aspect of advice is that there is almost always something missing at the start of it. Advice is most often given in the form of 'What you need to do is…' when it more accurately needs to be stated as 'If I were you I would …'. Now don't get me wrong here, there are times when good advice falls upon fertile ground and the results are life changing. This possibility is one of the reasons why I buy a lotto entry every week – one day the numbers might be right for me! Sadly, to date they haven't been, and while most advice will be right for the person offering it, it will rarely be within the perceptual funnel of the person hearing it. It is my belief that we can never know another person well enough to give them realistic advice. The provision of information is a reasonable aim, unless it is provided with the expectation that the other person will understand it, integrate it into their perceptual funnel, and act on it.

The third factor that frustrates advice giving is the concept of 'shooting the messenger'. If the person dispensing the advice is seen by us as a credible source then we might be open to that advice. This is one of the reasons that advertisers use celebrities and people in white coats in their advertisements. Anyone who remembers the reaction of the brands that were paying Tiger Woods millions for his endorsements at the time of his very public marriage breakdown will see that the credibility of the messenger is vital to the message being accepted. If we don't value the credibility of the messenger then there is little chance that we will find their message credible.

These three factors will almost always interfere with the recipient's ability to 'take good advice'.

In a personal example, I have been around 15kg above my ideal weight for most of my forty adult years. A very dear friend, upon hearing that I was once again exploring a change of eating habits, raised the topic of calories in versus calories out. Now this man was skinny, so you would imagine that he was a relative authority on nutrition and exercise. It occurred to me, however, to explore with him his dietary and fitness regimen. He readily admitted that he had never exercised a day in his life and he considered a balanced meal to include chocolate and ice cream. In other words, he was dispensing advice which he had never needed to take. This conversation happened around twenty years ago and he is still skinny, while I am still slightly overweight! I know that he was giving me good advice, it was not even news to me, unfortunately it was not within my ability to accept it – it was outside my perceptual funnel, and he was not a credible source.

As a result, our Auto Pilot can filter out a lot of the good advice and feedback from those around us, and some of us can struggle to receive this advice and feedback even if we have requested it, as mentioned earlier in this chapter. This is why a therapeutic relationship can often deliver outcomes and changes that are very rare in more traditional human relationships.

As a psychologist I have always been very aware of the limitations of my profession. We have almost no capacity to change our client's environment or circumstances, we are usually limited to the world view that our client provides us, and we are given a mere fifty minutes each week or two to try to make a difference.

However, the therapeutic relationship is still a very powerful one, and is regulated very heavily in most parts of the world for this reason.

The power of the therapeutic relationship includes the following points.

We have no history with our client, and therefore there are few preconceptions and bad habits to get in the way. There is no emotional connection between the therapist and the client, which means that the client's Auto Pilot has not yet developed filters to block or distort our observations and recommendations. We have a limited future with a client, which means that our motives are relatively pure. Our agenda is single-mindedly focused on our client's wellbeing (or it should be if we are acting ethically), and our needs as therapists are firmly in second place. Additionally, the potential for any harmful agenda is limited, so the client's Auto Pilot is more relaxed and open. Finally, therapists typically have some expertise and experience, so are perceived by the client's Auto Pilot as credible and powerful.

By contrast, normal relationships have a history which has trained both Auto Pilots in the idiosyncrasies of the other party. (Consequently, the Auto Pilot holds the ridiculous belief that it can read the other person's mind.) There is usually a strong emotional connection (good or bad) in a normal relationship which activates the Auto Pilot and creates misconceptions and programmed beliefs regarding the other person's credibility and motives. Most normal relationships are intended, by at least one party, to be long term and therefore hold the potential for conflicting agendas.

Finally, I have yet to meet a troubled couple who have been trained in relationship management, conflict resolution, and mutually considering each other's needs. Most parties in a normal relationship are almost profoundly ignorant regarding the theoretical and practical management of an adult relationship. It is not taught in school and our Auto Pilot learnt almost all of its relationship programming when it was a child. Thus, the perceptions and accuracy of that knowledge are both flawed and corrupted, compounded by the fact that all of our parents were on Auto Pilot when they were raising us!

This is one of the reasons why we 'ignore' the good advice and honest input of the people who routinely populate our lives. It is unsettling to consider how many times a client has immediately understood and 'owned' something that I have mentioned in therapy and their supportive spouse has shaken their head and said, 'That's what I have been telling you for years!' This is a perfectly normal and understandable phenomenon when considered in light of the two brains metaphor. On the occasions when a partner is a 'fly on the wall' in therapy, it is almost always because they are supportive and engaged. My clients typically report that they are seeking to improve their communication and to make the people they love happier. Unfortunately, the length of their relationship and the amount of emotional engagement they have achieved have combined to allow their Auto Pilot to develop habitual patterns of behaviour regarding those they love. Their Auto Pilot has developed some very powerful techniques of filtering out the input of these people. Then they engage in therapy. Just like my experience with seeing the video of my golf game for the first time, their Auto Pilot is presented with irrefutable evidence that their perceptions of themselves are inaccurate.

An example is the toilet seat problem. Households all over the world are bedevilled by the divide between the 'seat up' and 'seat down' supporters.

Now there does exist a mealy mouthed justification to support the 'seat up' proponents. That argument is that the 'seat down' supporters are capable of closing the lid if they really want the seat lid to be down. While this is an emotional and valueless argument, it is one which my Auto Pilot used for over forty years. Then one day my Clever Brain finally came into play and I realised that there were two values-based considerations that my Auto Pilot had not even contemplated. One was my value of living in a hygienic environment, and the other was living in a harmonious environment. Once again I had an 'Oh no!' moment when I realised that I had allowed my habitual behaviour to override my values.

I was aware from my time as a sales rep to hospitals that aerosol contamination was a serious source of infection and potential harm. I also realised that the high levels of agitation that flushing a toilet produced would allow the contaminated water to produce aerosols. These are the minute droplets that float in the air and potentially contain bacteria and microbes – all round pretty yucky! So why would I deliberately leave the seat up and permit such noxious materials to float uninterrupted through my home? I was also aware of the old adage 'happy spouse, happy house', and my wonderful wife was a 'seat down' enthusiast. Why then would I act in such a disagreeable and uncooperative manner over something so trivial? These realisations caused me to review my behaviour and, over time, teach my Auto Pilot to close the lid. Now, how to teach my son to do it? Any suggestions?

If you find your Auto Pilot is struggling to process and respond to feedback from those you have empowered to influence your Auto Pilot, a therapist might be a viable alternative. In a therapeutic relationship you can get this feedback in a way that is seen as more objective and more qualified, and therefore more likely to be accepted by your Auto Pilot.

Chapter summary

- The way we perceive ourselves is almost never accurate as our Auto Pilot is willing to delude us into thinking what it believes we want to know. This is why it's important to ask others for feedback.

- However, advice doesn't always work, even when we request it. We have a tendency to miss good advice because it is outside our perceptual funnel, or we see it as unrealistic for our personal circumstances, or we don't see the person giving the advice in a very credible light. These problems unfortunately mean well-intentioned help can sometimes backfire.

- Therapeutic relationships can often deliver outcomes and changes that are very rare in more traditional human relationships.   .

GREAT
((CHANGE))
MAKER

WHY CLEVER PEOPLE
DO DUMB THINGS

CHAPTER 9:

ENJOY A RICH, FULL AND MEANINGFUL LIFE

This book is a collaborative endeavour, bringing therapeutic frameworks, metaphors, and my own thoughts and experiences to the page. If that is where they stay then nothing will change. This is why the ultimate benefit of this book lies in what you decide to do with it.

In my psychology practice I have seen thousands of clients profoundly change their own sense of wellbeing without actually changing anything concrete in their lives. I have taken statistics across hundreds of completed client relationships. The average Outcome Rating Scale at the beginning of our work together was 16.7 out of 40, and the average at the end of our work together was 32.7 out of 40.

The difference between these ratings was not necessarily related to circumstances. Clearly people living under threat of war or famine will report lowered wellbeing, and measures of world happiness (The Happiness Report, for example) show that stability and autonomy strongly contribute to happiness. The reason is that these social elements complement our Auto Pilot's requirements. Our Auto Pilot is incapable of solving problems, and this means that stability, particularly over time, is likely to lead to Auto Pilot programming that is conducive to feelings of happiness and contentment. Autonomy, the right to make our own decisions, is also likely to have a long-term beneficial effect on our wellbeing. If our Auto Pilot has been socially programmed to function in a stable environment where people feel that they are in control of their own lives, then wellbeing is almost certainly going to increase.

However, the point I want to make is that, once these basic requirements of stability and autonomy have been met, you don't need to change your circumstances to live a rich, full and meaningful life. When I look at my clients, none of them reported winning the lotto, and very few of them gained their dream job, or found a nicer person to be their partner, or threw their kids out of the house, or … you get the picture.

Instead, these people found a way to change the way they think about the way they think.

What if I don't 'get it'?

In my practice as a psychologist I have heard many stories of people who have sought professional help and have still been left feeling helpless and dissatisfied. They typically report that either the personality fit or the approach of the therapist just did not work for them. I have no doubt that some of my clients have been left feeling the same way. Some of these people walked away from therapy, others soldiered on wondering when it might make a difference to them. The reality is that no single approach or therapist is going to work for everyone.

Instead, to make changes, there is a need for 'therapeutic rapport', that state of mind where both parties are cooperating, where neither side feels significant antagonism towards the other, and where some progress is being attained.

The same is true for this book, and whether or not you 'get' the content I've shared here comes down to the same factors that will determine whether or not a certain therapist's or practitioner's advice 'works' for you.

In therapy, when it does 'work' and my clients do 'get it', it's usually a case of serendipity, or the right person at the right time. I suspect that these people were already on the edge of a breakthrough but lacked the information, strategies and support to be able to make that breakthrough.

I recall a recent experience where a young woman came to me on the personal recommendation of a friend and the referral of her GP. She openly admitted that she had been to a number of counsellors and felt that it was a waste of time. After gaining an insight into her life we began discussing the model presented in this book. As we worked through the Influence Diagram she suddenly said, 'All my life I have felt that there were two of me. A powerful me who made a lot of mistakes, and a real me who knew better. Now I think I understand.' This is clearly a case of the stars aligning. Rather than any of the other professionals with whom this young lady had worked being wrong or providing bad advice, she and I simply met when she was already on the edge of that breakthrough, and the information we discussed was the final piece of the puzzle.

So if you don't quite 'get it', then perhaps it isn't the right time. Perhaps I'm not the right person, or perhaps my style or approach offends or confuses you. If this is the case, then please speak up! Go to my website and join a forum, listen to a podcast or engage in a webinar (your first webinar is free if you own a copy of this book). If none of this helps then I will gladly refund what you spent on this book (details of my refund policy are available on my website www.greatchangemaker. com.au/guarantee).

I 'GET IT', BUT IT'S NOT WORKING YET...

If you're like the majority of my clients, then you probably feel comfortable with the model and are embracing the struggle to make it happen in your daily life. You'll feel a sense of accomplishment when you avoid an 'Oh no!' moment, and delight when you realise you're recognising more and more 'Oh wow!' moments.

Or you might feel a sense of accomplishment after reading this book, but then lapse back under the control of your Auto Pilot and wonder why you are back to square one.

Or you might 'get it' but struggle with implementation. When working with clients, some sessions will have the feel of Groundhog Day, the movie where the journalist relives a particular day until he resolves his big life issues.

When frustration emerges, remember that you have been under the invisible influence of your Auto Pilot for your entire life prior to reading this book. I personally thought I had my eye on the ball in tennis. I also thought I had a smooth golf swing. In both cases it wasn't until I saw external evidence, that I realised my Auto Pilot was tricking me into believing I was 'perfect' when I most certainly was not.

If you think you 'get it' but are struggling to implement this knowledge (or to implement it consistently), remember that making deliberate change is hard. You have spent your entire life to date unwittingly allowing your Auto Pilot to run your life. The fact that it has done such a great job overall has almost nothing to do with you. It has to do with the feedback you have been receiving from your environment. You have been taking advice and direction from other people, the media, your parents and friends, your entire life. The way you dress and wear your hair, whether you use perfume or cologne, whether your smoke or consume alcohol, are all part of the environment you have been exposed to your entire life.

Fortunately your Auto Pilot is very trainable, and the more you do it, the easier it gets. Try to slow down and be mindful before you act. Make an effort to make big decisions mindfully. Be open to being confused, and use tools like writing and Dream Sheets to awaken your Clever Brain. Give your Auto Pilot clear instructions about what you want, recognising what he does well, and redirecting him when necessary. The more you do these things, the closer you will be to living a rich, full and meaningful life.

WHAT YOU CAN EXPECT

If the idea of having a powerful but stupid Auto Pilot, and an intelligent but lazy Clever Brain, has resonated with you, then you are on the way to developing new habitual patterns of thought which will lead you towards a richer, fuller, and more meaningful life. As you free yourself from the inherent limitations of your habitual and emotional Auto Pilot, and access the intelligence and creativity of your Clever Brain, you will live a life more aligned with your values. You will be more comfortable experiencing and expressing your genuine confusion over the things in and around you which do not appear to work. You will have begun to slow down your reactions and emotional responses to deliberately influence them in moving towards your values rather than away from them. You will start viewing the reactions of other people in a very different light as you realise that they are not in control of what they do, think and say. You will be mindfully accepting that most people are being controlled by of their Auto Pilot, and that this is a reasonable explanation of why they do stupid, inconsiderate and dangerous things.

If you embrace the ideas in this book then you will continue to have a life that includes adversity. Pain, loss, hardship, anger, disappointment, and even resentment, are all parts of life. Awakening your Clever Brain does not make these things go away or feel any better. What your Clever Brain can do is put these things in the context of your entire life. While awful, these things are events, rather than a definition of your life. The ugly emotions that adversity can generate are real. However, the need to intensely hold on to those emotions for the rest of your life is not real. Grief is a legitimate expression of loss and love, and experiencing grief after losing a loved one is an important part of loving them and their memory. Being bullied is a horrible experience, and anger and resentment over such an experience is normal and reasonable. But ruminating over it for the rest of your life is your Auto Pilot's way of permitting the bully to maintain that power over you. Ask yourself, what would your unemotional and logical Clever Brain want you to do?

In my case, in the years since discovering this liberating and empowering approach to life, I have developed the opinion that I am the luckiest man in the world. I do appreciate that my claim to that title might easily be challenged. After all, I have a pile of stuff that contains some pretty significant items. However, what this approach has delivered for me and many of my clients is constant access to the entire pile of stuff, including everything in that pile that works for me.

A rich, full, and meaningful life is a wonderful gift for you to give yourself, and it will enrich the lives of those around you. While it will not be a perfect life, it will be a life which is moving towards perfection.

In closing...

Thank you for reading my book. I have tried very hard to have my Clever Brain influence its content. You may well have found examples throughout this book which demonstrate the power that an Auto Pilot can have, even when a Clever Brain is highly activated. If I only had the power to change one thing in you, my reader, it would be to allow you to develop the firm and legitimate belief that you are the luckiest person in the world. It is this belief that will allow you to be as happy and successful on the inside as I sincerely hope that you are on the outside. To deliberately misquote Spock from Star Trek, 'Think well and prosper!'

Regards,

GREAT
(« *CHANGE* »)
MAKER

RESOURCES

Hopefully this book is the continuation of a process in your journey towards a rich, full and meaningful life – a process of expanding your own funnel and increasing your own perceptions. To continue expanding your perceptual funnel and awakening your Clever Brain, I recommend you look at the following resources.

ACT

There is a very active Acceptance and Commitment Theory (ACT) community online at contextualscience.org. Originated by Stephen Hayes, PhD, ACT is a philosophy which encourages openness and experimentation.

You will find that the ACT framework is described in very different terms to most of those used in this book. The beauty of ACT is that it is not locked in to a specific vernacular or framework. As you explore the wider ACT community you will find that the differences are in description and interpretation rather than disagreement. *ACT Made Simple* by Stephen Hayes and *The Happiness Trap* by Russ Harris are superb explorations of the framework. Russ Harris has written a number of books and *ACT with Love* is a brilliant resource for couples.

The Five Languages of Love

There is an elegant but unscientific approach to communicating within relationships created by Dr Gary Chapman called *The Five Languages of Love*. It is available on the internet www.5lovelanguages.com and your local library will have books you can borrow if needed. This simple framework describes different communication styles, is easy to understand, and is an elegant way to awaken both parties' Clever Brains. A link to 5 languages of love is also available through my webpage www.greatchangemaker.com.au/CleverPeople

Great Change Maker

Visit my website, www.greatchangemaker.com for blogs, webinars and other online resources, as well as to share your comments and feedback on this book.

I have also begun to offer group and individual resources and sessions outside of my private practice in Ipswich, Queensland. This includes keynote speaking, individual and group mentoring, and seminars worldwide.

Why Clever People Do Dumb Things

For resources specific to this book please visit www.greatchangemaker.com.au/CleverPeople This is where you will find worksheets; links; miscellaneous resources along with other bonus material.

ABOUT THE AUTHOR

Lindsay Spencer-Matthews has been a registered psychologist for over 20 years and in that time he has helped thousands of people change the way they think about the way they think. Driven by a desire to help more than the people he was able to see in his private practice, Lindsay wrote this book and embarked on a new chapter of his long and successful career.

Lindsay now offers keynote speaking, seminars and mentoring as well as continuing to see some clients in his private practice. His keynotes are delivered in a light hearted conversational style which allows his audiences to embrace powerful new concepts whilst remaining just within their comfort zones. His seminars are filled with fun and practical experiences which allow participants to bring their own experiences and knowledge to bear on novel and effective techniques to change the way they think and act. His mentoring brings the authority and experience of a successful forty year career with clients uniformly reporting their appreciation of his impact on their working and personal lives.

Some of the topics available in the 'Clever' series includes:

Why Clever Managers Do Dumb Things
Why Clever Staff Do Dumb Things
Why Clever Customers Do Dumb Things
Why Clever Spouses Do Dumb Things
Why Clever Professionals And Business Owners Do Dumb Things
Why Clever Therapists Do Dumb Things

To explore these opportunities with Lindsay please visit

www.greatchangemaker.com.au

#CLEVERPEOPLE

See the competition page on how to win exclusive
Why Clever People Do Dumb Things prizes
using our hashtag #CleverPeople

www.greatchangemaker.com.au
(join our mailing list for updates, useful
and free resources)

Do something clever . . . .

Win an exclusive prize.

**WHY CLEVER PEOPLE
DO DUMB THINGS**

To be in the running just take a photo of you reading your copy of the book in situ*. Upload your photo to social media using hashtag #CleverPeople

The best photo each month will win a limited edition 'Clever People' coffee mug (or similar).

*Feel free to be creative and have fun
but please keep your photos tasteful and clean.

Check into the Great Change Maker's website

www.greatchangemaker.com.au

for the latest information on prizes and competition details

WE ARE ALL BORN AS A BLANK SLATE AND WE THEN SPEND OUR LIVES BECOMING THE PERSON WE BECOME. SADLY MUCH OF THAT DEVELOPMENT IS DONE COMPLETELY BY ACCIDENT!

WE LEARN ATTITUDES, REACTIONS, HABITS, AND RESPONSES WITHOUT REALISING WHAT WE ARE DOING!

CONTACT GREAT CHANGE MAKER TO FIND OUT ABOUT OUR MOTIVATIONAL SPEAKING, WORKSHOPS AND MENTORING SESSIONS!

#CLEVERPEOPLE
Web - www.greatchangemaker.com.au
(join our mailing list for updates & free resources)
Email - info@greatchangemaker.com.au
FACEBOOK – GREATCHANGEMAKER
TWITTER – GR8CHANGEMAKER
LINKEDIN – LINDSAY SPENCER-MATTHEWS

www.ingramcontent.com/pod-product-compliance
Lightning Source LLC
Chambersburg PA
CBHW071445090426
42737CB00011B/1789